PROPHETS OF THE NEW TESTAMENT

Before, During, and After Jesus

KIERAN LARKIN

Prophets of the New Testament

Copyright © 2023 by Kieran Larkin

Published by Red Penguin Books

All rights reserved.

Published by Red Penguin Books

Bellerose Village, New York

ISBN

Print 978-1-63777-494-6

Digital 978-1-63777-493-9

No part of this book may be reproduced in any form or by any electronic or mechanical means, including information storage and retrieval systems, without written permission from the author, except for the use of brief quotations in a book review.

CONTENTS

Preface	v
1. The Role of the New Testament Prophet	1
2. Zechariah and Elizabeth	9
3. Simeon and Anna	17
4. John the Baptist	27
5. Barnabas	47
6. Simeon Niger, Lucius, and Manaen	61
7. Agabus	75
8. Judas Barsabbas and Silas	83
9. Saul (Paul) of Tarsus	95
10. John of Patmos	151
11. Philip the Evangelist and His Four Daughters	199
12. The Twelve	217
Bibliography	229
About the Author	235

PREFACE

Elijah was called the "Father of the Prophets." Amos has been christened the "Prophet of Social Justice." Jeremiah is known as the "Reluctant Prophet." In the Academy Award-winning film *Network*, television anchorman Howard Beale was advertised as the "Mad Prophet of the Airwaves." All of these—and many, many more men and women throughout the ages—have been defined or described as *prophets*. This begs the question: who *is* a prophet?

This volume completes a trilogy I began four years ago when I wrote *Messengers of God: A Survey of Old Testament Prophets,* and followed it with *Women Prophets of the Old Testament,* two years later. I have long admired the prophets of the *Old Testament*—both men and women—for their great devotion to God, their willingness to answer His call, and the trials and tribulations (often incredibly severe) they accepted as part and parcel of the ministry they agreed to undertake. I considered it an honor to chronicle and celebrate their faith, dedication and courage.

The composition of these first two books required a fair amount of research—research I was only too happy to undertake in that it taught me a great deal about a group of individuals I truly admired. The effort is never too great when you can tangibly see and feel the fruits of your labor and their positive contributions to your life. But in embarking on this new, but related, venture—tackling the prophets of the *New* Testament—I felt as if I were completely in over my head. Were there *really* prophets in the *New Testament* besides John the Baptist? Didn't the coming of Jesus in fulfillment of so many of the *Old Testament* prophecies bring the necessity for more prophets to an end? I didn't think I could name even one additional prophet in the New Testament—if there was one! It turns out that there are really quite a few—depending, of course, on what you consider a prophet to be. But in many cases, attempting to present a proper treatment of their lives, ministries, and messages is incredibly difficult because the details are so maddeningly scant.

In writing about the prophets of the *Old Testament*, I learned that their primary function—first and foremost—was to deliver messages from God to the people of Israel and Judah. Predictions about future events, which so many wrongly believed to be central to prophethood, are not necessarily center-stage in prophetic ministry. To the extent that so many *Old Testament* predictions focused on the arrival of God's Messiah, when the Messiah eventually arrived in the *New Testament*—as we believe as Christians—did prophets lose their purpose and become superfluous? Or...did their function change? It was to these questions that I had to direct my energy and seek possible answers.

It is my hope in this book to compare and contrast the respective responsibilities of the prophets who have been so identified in each of the two Testaments—Old and New. But this has proven to be no easy task. There seems to be little to no agreement on the part of theologians and Biblical scholars as to the identity of the New Testament prophets, invariably due to the fact that there is such widespread *dis*agreement as to the function and role of "prophets" immediately before the birth of Jesus, during His years of public ministry, and in the days following His Crucifixion, Resurrection and Ascension. While some individuals may be referred to as "prophets" in the corpus of the New Testament, the appropriateness of that designation is the subject of ongoing debate—two thousand years later!

I think it is only fitting that I begin this discussion of prophethood by using as a baseline the generic definition that a prophet serves first and foremost as a *messenger for God*, a spokesperson who conveys His message(s) to whichever audience He chooses. Almost all of the *New Testament* prophets discussed in this text meet that criteria: they are specifically called "prophets," even if in some cases the messages they have been asked to deliver are not articulated scripturally. In some cases, their prophetic ministry may be far less verbal and much more behavioral. As you will see, a number of reputable theologians, in reviewing the efforts of those men and women called prophets, have expressed the belief that the role of the prophet in the New Testament may have evolved into a function quite different from the delivery of a divine message, as was the norm in the Old Testament. In this case, I think, these theologians must simply "agree to disagree."

I should also mention my frustration in presenting a *New Testament* figure to my reading audience as a "prophet," yet I am unable to specify exactly what message that figure has been told by God to deliver to His People. It's like calling a person a baseball player without ever having seen him/her play in a game.

As a high school teacher of religious studies in a Catholic academy for young women, I use the *Good News Bible (with Deuterocanonicals/Apocrypha)* in my class discussions because I favor its contemporary translation. Published by the American Bible Society, its imprimatur was granted by Archbishop John Francis Whealon of Hartford, Connecticut. This is the primary translation I will use throughout this text. In saying this, I also realize that different translators of the New Testament may express their translations differently, and that that will sometimes make a difference.

Chapter One

THE ROLE OF THE NEW TESTAMENT PROPHET

How does one determine if another is a prophet without understanding what a prophet is? And if there is little agreement on this definition, how much more difficult will that determination be? It is common knowledge that the *New Testament* was written by a number of different authors at different times in different places to different reading audiences about different issues (of course, the same can be said about the prophets of the *Old Testament* as well!) So is it possible to arrive at an agreement as to the role of the prophet in order to identify those who fill this role? This needs to be the logical starting point in order to determine who belongs on the roster of *New Testament* prophets.

Dr. Richard Blaylock of the Biblical Studies Department of Western Seminary in Northern California pointed out in his 2022 Gospel Coalition monograph in the journal *Themelios* that "prophecy remains an elusive concept among academics...Scholars have yet to reach a consensus regarding what the *New Testament* prophets were actually doing when they were prophesying." He went on to outline five different theories about the purpose behind the writings and ministries of the recognized prophets of the *New Testament*: interpretation of Scripture, pastoral preaching, Gospel proclamation, interpretation of revelation and mediation with the world of spirits. While Blaylock provides a depthful summary of the thought process other theologians have presented in support of each of these theories, he rejects them one by one as being incomplete, primarily because they cannot be tied to each example of prophetic action found in the *New Testament*. But let's take a look at each of these theories.

The idea that the *interpretation of Scripture* was a key component of *New Testament* prophecy was espoused by the renowned Professor of Biblical Interpretation Christopher R. Seitz at Wycliffe College of the University of Toronto. Seitz explained in his book *Prophecy and Hermeneutics: Toward a New Introduction to the Prophets* that "The interpretation of Scripture, usually in the synagogues, is a key feature of the missions of the prophets Paul and Barnabas, Paul and Silas, as well as of Peter and other Christian leaders. This manner of teaching is elaborated in *Acts* 13:16-41 in the form of a synagogue homily. It may or may not be significant that the 'prophets' in question are also 'teachers.'"

Baptist pastor and theologian David Hill has equated the role of prophet with that of *pastoral preacher,* citing (among other sources) St. Paul's *First Letter to the Corinthians*:

> *But the one who proclaims God's message speaks to people and gives them help, encouragement and comfort. The one who speaks in strange tongues helps only himself, but the one who proclaims God's message helps the whole church. (1 Corinthians 14:3-4)*

Dr. James L. Boyer of Grace Theological Seminary, in his 1960 *Grace Journal* article "The Office of the Prophet in New Testament Times," echoed this sentiment when he wrote "John [the Baptist] preached repentance for the sins of his day as well as announcing the advent of the Messiah, and it was this preaching which earned him the reputation of a prophet with the people."

Prophecy is thought also by some to be closely related to the *proclamation of the Gospel message*. The Greek word *kerygma*, translated into English as "proclamation," refers, according to Roman Catholic Archbishop Christophe Pierre, to "the joyful announcement that Jesus Christ is a living Person to be encountered Who, through His Resurrection, has defeated sin and death." Rev. Thomas W. Gillespie, former president of Princeton Theological Seminary, maintained that *New Testament* prophecy, especially as found in the ministrations of St. Paul, is intimately connected with such proclamations as:

> *No one can confess 'Jesus is Lord' unless he is guided by the Holy Spirit. (1 Corinthians 12:3)*

Professors of Biblical Studies Terrance Callan of the Athenaeum and Wayne Grudem of Trinity Evangelical Divinity School viewed prophecy as the *hearing and interpretation of an interior "voice"*—different from one's own and emanating from God—that must then be properly and personally interpreted before being expressed to others. However, this viewpoint seems to clash with the words of Peter, who said:

> *No one can explain by himself a prophecy in the Scriptures. For no prophetic message ever came just from the will of man, but men were under the control of the Holy Spirit as they spoke the message that came from God. (2 Peter 1:20-21)*

And finally, Dr. Clint Tibbs of Catholic University, whose area of expertise is related to the grammar, pronunciation and interpretation of the original languages of Scripture, offered a unique understanding of prophecy as "the gift of *becoming a medium through whom spirits can speak* the mother tongue of the spectators." Dr. Tibbs maintained that proper analysis of the Greek language in the New Testament suggested the presence of multiple spirits (rather than the one "Holy Spirit") who proclaimed Jesus through "possessing" prophets, who served as media through whom the spirits were able to communicate.

Ultimately, Dr. Blaylock offers his own definition, which he believes "covers all the bases" in a way that each of the previous interpretations was unable to accomplish. While a tad unwieldy, he suggests *"New Testament* prophecy can be defined as:

1. a miraculous act of intelligible communication,
2. rooted in spontaneous, divine revelation, and
3. empowered by the Holy Spirit, so that
4. the prophetic words spoken (or written) could be attributed to any and all members of the Godhead and which therefore
5. must be received by those who hear or read them as absolutely binding and true."

Certainly this very detailed definition offers a great deal of food for thought.

Dr. Boyer believes that, in terms of its function, prophecy in the *New Testament* is just a continuation of the prophecy of the *Old Testament*. However, he sees its function as containing four distinct elements: "the predictive element...the hortatory element...the possession of supernatural knowledge and...the power to perform miracles and wonders."

Pentecostal minister and televangelist Don Stewart expressed his view in much simpler terms, maintaining, "As was true in the *Old Testament* period, the main job of the *New Testament* prophets was to speak forth the word of God." This straightforward description was also supported by Dr. Sam Storms, pastor and founder of Enjoying God Ministries, when he wrote that "Many contend that prophecy under both covenants [*Old* and *New Testaments*] functioned in essentially the same way. Thus the *New Testament* prophet received inspired words from God, and what he declared was equal in authority as, say, of Isaiah or Amos."

So where does this leave us? So many reputable, accomplished, committed, inspired and scholarly theologians all reading the same scriptural passages, all praying and discerning what they have read—and all coming away with different viewpoints and conclusions. Is there one definitive, incontrovertible understanding of the exact role played by the individuals identified as prophets throughout the corpus of the *New Testament*? If such an assemblage of competent and highly educated, highly qualified theologians cannot come to an agreement, then the only alternative is to "agree to disagree"—and offer a presentation of each individual so described, with the realization that substantial supporting data and/or explanation of why these prophets are prophets indeed—will sometimes be in very short supply.

CHAPTER 1: QUESTIONS FOR REVIEW

1. Do the prophets of the *New Testament* play the same role as the prophets of the *Old Testament*?
2. What are five different theories espoused by theologians about the ministries and purposes of the prophets of the *New Testament*?
3. What is meant by the Greek word *kerygma*—and how does it apply to the prophets of the *New Testament*?
4. What definition of *New Testament* prophecy is offered by Dr. Richard Blaylock?

Chapter Two

ZECHARIAH AND ELIZABETH

*"Zechariah was filled with the Holy Spirit,
and he spoke God's message..."*
*"Why should this great thing happen to me, that my
Lord's mother comes to visit me?"*

Zechariah was a descendant of Moses' brother Aaron, and thus served—as did all of Aaron's posterity—in the priesthood of Judea. He belonged to the clan of Abijah, one of the 24 priestly clans that took turns in administering the Temple in Jerusalem. According to Biblical author Jack Zavala, each of these clans rotated in their service to the Temple for periods of one week's time twice each year. Zechariah's wife was Elizabeth, also a descendant of Aaron, and both were advanced in years (their ages unknown) and were never blessed with children.

The story of Zechariah and Elizabeth appears only in the Gospel of St. Luke, insofar as only Luke and Matthew record events connected with the life of the infant Jesus. Luke extolled the virtuous life of this couple:

> *They both lived good lives in God's sight and obeyed fully all the Lord's laws and commands. (Luke 1:6)*

But there is much more to their story than that. Their personal relationship also exuded a love and trust not only in God, but in each other as well. As Sue and Larry Richards explained in their 1999 text *Every Woman in the Bible*, "Elizabeth and Zechariah had a warm and loving relationship. They were old and childless. If Zechariah had not loved his wife, her childlessness would have been grounds for divorce and remarriage. Yet, through many long years the two had clung together." The Richards went on to point out that "Despite the couple's age, Zechariah had not ceased praying for a child, which was so important to every Jewish woman. Zechariah's continuing prayer indicates not only his love for Elizabeth but also the couple's continuing trust in God."

ZECHARIAH'S DOUBT AND DUMBNESS

Divine revelation and possession of supernatural knowledge and its transmission to others—two of the hallmarks of prophecy mentioned in Chapter 1—came to Zechariah as he went about his ministerial work as a Temple priest:

> *One day Zechariah was doing his work as a priest in the Temple, taking his turn in the daily service. According to the custom followed by the priests, he was chosen by lot to burn incense on the altar. So he went into the Temple of the Lord, while the crowd of people outside prayed during the hour when the incense was burned. An angel of the Lord appeared to him, standing at the right side of the altar where the incense was burned. When Zechariah saw him, he was alarmed and felt afraid. But the angel said to him, "Don't be afraid, Zechariah! God has heard your prayer, and your wife Elizabeth will bear you a son. You are to name him John. How glad and happy you will be, and how happy many others will be when he is born! He will be a great man in the Lord's sight. He must not drink any wine or strong drink. From his very birth he will be filled with the Holy Spirit, and he will bring back many of the people of Israel to the Lord their God. He will go ahead of the Lord, strong and mighty like the prophet Elijah. He will bring fathers and children together again; he will turn disobedient people back to the way of thinking of the righteous; he will get the Lord's people ready for Him."*

> Zechariah said to the angel, "How shall I know if this is so? I am an old man, and my wife is old also."
>
> "I am Gabriel," the angel answered. "I stand in the presence of God, Who sent me to speak to you and tell you this good news. But you have not believed my message, which will come true at the right time. Because you have not believed, you will be unable to speak; you will remain silent until the day my promise to you comes true."
>
> In the meantime the people were waiting for Zechariah and wondering why he was spending such a long time in the Temple. When he came out, he could not speak to them, and so they knew that he had seen a vision in the Temple. Unable to say a word, he made signs to them with his hands. (Luke 1:8-22)

ELIZABETH'S FAITH

After Gabriel's revelation to Zechariah, the scene then shifted to his wife Elizabeth. It is unknown how much time elapsed between the visitation of Gabriel to Zechariah and the advent of Elizabeth's pregnancy—Scripture simply says *"Some time later..." (Luke 1:24)*, but it was in the sixth month of Elizabeth's pregnancy that Gabriel then visited Mary in Nazareth to announce God's plan for her to give birth to the *"Son of the Most High God." (Luke 1:32)* It was in this "Annunciation" that Gabriel revealed to Mary that her much older relative (cousin?) Elizabeth—thought to be infertile—had become pregnant in her advanced years. Mary then took it upon herself to visit Elizabeth, who greeted her with words that indicated that she, too, had received a divine revelation:

You are the most blessed of all women, and blessed is the child you will bear! Why should this great thing happen to me, that my Lord's mother comes to visit me? For as soon as I heard your greeting, the baby within me jumped with gladness. How happy are you to believe that the Lord's message to you will come true! (Luke 1:42-45)

After Elizabeth gave birth, and the time arrived eight days later to circumcise and name her son, Elizabeth broke with the tradition of naming the child after a relative, and announced that the child was to be named "John." (Unknown to the assemblage, Gabriel had told Zechariah at the Temple visitation to name the child John.) When those present sought verification from Zechariah about the child's name, Zechariah, still unable to speak, wrote "his name is John." At this moment his power of speech was returned to him:

John's father Zechariah was filled with the Holy Spirit, and he spoke God's message:

"Let us praise the Lord, the God of Israel! He has come to the help of His people and has set them free.

He has provided for us a mighty Savior, a descendant of His servant David.

He promised through His holy prophets long ago that He would save us from our enemies, from the power of all those who hate us.

He said He would show mercy to our ancestors and remember His sacred covenant.

> *With a solemn oath to our ancestor Abraham He promised to rescue us from our enemies and allow us to serve Him without fear, so that we might be holy and righteous before Him all the days of our life.*
>
> *You, my child, will be called a prophet of the Most High God.*
>
> *You will go ahead of the Lord to prepare His road for Him, to tell His people that they will be saved by having their sins forgiven.*
>
> *Our God is merciful and tender.*
>
> *He will cause the bright dawn of salvation to rise on us and to shine from heaven on all those who live in the dark shadow of death, to guide our steps into the path of peace."* (Luke 1:68-79)

Zechariah's prophetic declaration above has been called "Zechariah's Canticle," or the "Benedictus," ever since, and is intoned at Lauds each day in the recitation of the Divine Office.

The significance of the prophethood of both Zechariah and Elizabeth lies in their reception of divine knowledge in the time immediately preceding the birth of the Messiah. Like the prophets of the Old Testament who were gifted with the ability to predict future events, in many cases references to the long-awaited Messiah, not only were they granted the revelation of what was to unfold in salvation history in the immediate future, but bestowed on them was the privilege of parenting the greatest prophet to precede the Messiah—John the Baptist. And more than that, both Zechariah and Elizabeth were given the opportunity to share with others the divine revelation with which they had been gifted.

CHAPTER 2: QUESTIONS FOR REVIEW

1. What evidence suggests that there was a strong, loving relationship between Zechariah and Elizabeth?
2. What were the circumstances under which Zechariah was told of God's plans for him and his wife?
3. Why was Zechariah's power of speech taken from him?
4. What words of Elizabeth allow for her to be considered a prophetess?
5. What predictions are made by Zechariah in his "Benedictus?"

Chapter Three
SIMEON AND ANNA

*"Lord, You have kept Your promise...with my own eyes
I have seen Your salvation"*
*"A very old prophetess, a widow named Anna...
spoke about the Child..."*

While Zechariah and Elizabeth, kinsfolk of Mary, were blessed with the revelation of the Messiah even before His Incarnation, Simeon and Anna were privileged to encounter the Messiah in the earliest days of His infancy.

Ancient Mosaic law, as found in the Book of *Leviticus*, considered a woman who gave birth to a son to be ritually impure for a total of forty days after childbirth. Accordingly, when that time period had elapsed, she was required to undergo a ritual of purification as well as make two offerings before being considered ritually clean:

> *The Lord gave Moses the following regulations for the people of Israel. For seven days after a woman gives birth to a son, she is ritually unclean, as she is during her monthly period. On the eighth day, the child shall be circumcised. Then it will be 33 more days until she is ritually clean from her loss of blood; she must not touch anything that is holy or enter the sacred Tent until the time of her purification is completed...*

> *When the time of her purification is completed, whether for a son or daughter, she shall bring to the priest at the entrance of the Tent of the Lord's presence a one-year-old lamb for a burnt offering and a pigeon or a dove for a sin offering. The priest shall present her offering to the Lord and perform the ritual to take away her impurity, and she will be ritually clean. (Leviticus 12:2-7)*

It was at this ceremony of the purification of Mary and the presentation of the Child Jesus in the Temple in Jerusalem that the Holy Family encountered both Simeon and Anna.

SIMEON'S PATIENCE AND PROPHECY

Little is really known of the man called Simeon, and both he and Anna are only mentioned in the Gospel of *Luke*. About Simeon, Luke wrote:

> *At the time there was a man named Simeon living in Jerusalem. He was a good, God-fearing man and was waiting for Israel to be saved. (Luke 2:25)*

This description of Simeon says very little, but describes an individual who is morally upright *("good")*, observant of the Law of Moses *("God-fearing")* and both patient and trusting *("waiting for Israel to be saved")*. Tradition holds that he was most probably advanced in years as well. Clearly, then, his virtuous life was both recognized and rewarded by God, because:

> *The Holy Spirit was with him and had assured him that he would not die before he had seen the Lord's promised Messiah. (Luke 2:25-26)*

Luke's description of Simeon's arrival in the Temple and the words he spoke both to the Lord and then to Mary offer justification for designating Simeon as a prophet who both delivers the message of God as well as predicts future events:

> *Led by the Spirit, Simeon went into the Temple. When the parents brought the child Jesus into the Temple to do for Him what the Law required, Simeon took the child in his arms and gave thanks to God:*
>
> *"Now, Lord, You have kept Your promise, and You may let Your servant go in peace. With my own eyes I have seen Your salvation, which You have prepared in the presence of all peoples: A light to reveal Your will to the Gentiles and bring glory to Your people Israel." (Luke 2:27-32)*

After offering his gratitude to the Lord, Simeon then turned his attention to Mary and Joseph. After blessing them both, he made this solemn prediction to Mary:

> *This child is chosen by God for the destruction and the salvation of many in Israel. He will be a sign from God which many people will speak against and so reveal their secret thoughts. And sorrow, like a sharp sword, will break your own heart. (Luke 2:34-35)*

Charles Haddon Spurgeon was a famous nineteenth century Baptist homilist who was nicknamed the "Prince of Preachers" due to his large following and the great number of his sermons which are still in print over a century later. In discussing Simeon in 1865, Spurgeon wrote that "he was a 'devout' man... he possessed 'inward and spiritual grace.'" He posited that "Poor old Simeon had now become gray-headed; it is very possible that he had passed the usual period allotted to man's life; but he did not wish to die; he wished for 'the consolation of Israel.' He did not wish that the tabernacle of his body might be dissolved, but he did hope that, through the chinks of that old battered tabernacle of his, he might be able to see the Lord. Like the hoary-headed Christian of our times, he did not desire to die, but he did desire to 'be with Christ, which was far better.'"

Spurgeon envisioned that "Every morning he went up to the temple, saying to himself, 'Perhaps he will come today.' Each night when he went home he bent his knee, and said, 'O Lord, come quickly; even so, come quickly.' And yet, per adventure, that morning he went to the temple, little thinking, perhaps, the hour was at hand when he should see his Lord there; but there he was, brought in the arms of his mother, a little babe; and Simeon knew him...Do you not think you see him, when he held the babe in his arms? Why, the old man did not then want his staff to lean on; down it went, and both his arms grasped the child. He may have trembled a little, but the mother of Jesus was not afraid to trust her child to him. How young he felt! As young as when ten years ago he walked with light foot through the streets of Jerusalem. Scarce in heaven did old Simeon feel more happy than he did at that moment when he clasped the babe in his arms! Do you not think you see him? Joy is flashing from his eyes."

We know nothing of the early life of Simeon, so the special blessing given to him by God—to encounter the Messiah before he died—clearly indicates that his faith and trust in the Lord had not gone unnoticed—or unrewarded—by the Almighty.

ANNA'S GRATITUDE

It was on this same day of Mary's purification rite and the presentation of Jesus at the Temple that a similar blessing was bestowed on Anna in much the same way as it had been granted to Simeon. As with Simeon, the Gospel of Luke offers very little biographical information about Anna, albeit a tad more than that which was written about Simeon. Luke writes:

> *There was a very old prophetess, a widow named Anna, daughter of Phanuel of the tribe of Asher. She had been married for only seven years, and was now 84 years old. She never left the Temple; day and night she worshiped God, fasting and praying. That very same hour she arrived and gave thanks to God and spoke about the child to all who were waiting for God to set Jerusalem free. (Luke 2:36-38)*

This short citation about Anna includes information about her father and her tribe, but fails to mention her husband or children—if she had children. Luke identified her as a prophetess, although he did not define Simeon as a prophet, so there must have been other circumstances or characteristics in Anna's life that would have led to Luke's designation. Also, it is singular that Anna is said *never* to have left the Temple, but spent all of her time in prayer and fasting. Was she accorded living quarters at the Temple? Was she a woman of independent wealth and means? Who provided for any of her physical needs? There must have been something quite special about her that would have given her such total, uninterrupted access to the Temple.

Theology Professor Robin Gallaher Branch of North-West University in South Africa recently wrote in "Bible History Today" on the website of the Biblical Archaeology Society, "Luke's description of her lifestyle may be seen as eccentric today, and quite likely was considered so at the time. She never leaves the Temple (*Luke 2:37*). She worships night and day, fasting and praying. She is a workaholic, available 24/7. Yet her lifestyle evidently invigorates her, for she is mobile, articulate, alert, spiritually savvy and unselfish."

Professor Branch also pointed out that "Anna, this worship workaholic, sets her own hours, schedule, route and routine. Arguably she listens to God and prays as directed. Others recognize her as a prophetess. The work of prayer indeed characterizes a prophet, for God told Abimelech that Abraham was 'a prophet and he will pray for you' (*Genesis 20:7*). Anna knows fasting brings results. Biblical precedents include Esther's three-day fast before courageously approaching Xerxes (*Esther 4:15-16*), and the abstinence of Daniel and his three friends regarding the delicacies of King Nebuchadnezzar's table (*Daniel 1:12*)." Furthermore, "As a prophetess, Anna receives insight into things that normally remain hidden to ordinary people; she recognizes who this child is and tells of his significance to selected people in Jerusalem. Her actions affirm *Amos 3:7*: 'Surely the Sovereign Lord does nothing without revealing his plans to his servants, the prophets.'"

Kris Swiatocho, the Director of the Singles Network Ministries program, saw Anna as a heroic figure who ignored the prevailing assumptions and expectations of her day to go her own way: "Anna was not like most women of her time. She chose a different path. More than likely, after her husband's death, Anna would have been encouraged to get married again and have children. Anna, instead, chose to stay single. She chose to share her faith with as many people as she could. She chose to serve the Lord. She chose to fast and pray, worshiping the Lord day and night. She chose to tell them the news of the Savior that was coming, no matter how long it might be before he came. She knew her purpose and she didn't let anyone's opinions or comments keep her from it. Anna's choice would not only affect her life in an abundant way, but also the lives of others ever since."

One rather important bit of information about Anna is left totally to the imagination of the readership of Luke's Gospel. While Luke wrote (as cited above) that Anna *'gave thanks to God and spoke about the child to all who were waiting for God to set Jerusalem free"*—what exactly did Anna say to those around her? Did she label the child as the Messiah? Did she see the child as a future liberator who would free Jerusalem from Roman domination? As a prophetess, was she able to offer anything more specific about the child's future? It is unclear from Scripture whether or not Anna arrived on time to hear the words of Simeon, or arrived a short time later. What *is* clear, however, is that Anna immediately began to thank God upon seeing the Christ Child, while Simeon's first response was to prophesy about the Child's future. Therefore, whether it was the result of an intuitional sense or divine inspiration, Anna was gifted with the instinctive knowledge that the Child would indeed be instrumental in the "freeing" of Jerusalem—in whatever form that happened to take.

The significance of Simeon and Anna lies in the fact that they were the first individuals outside of the Christ Child's own family to have been gifted with foreknowledge of the identity and mission of the Messiah. Their recognition of the Child predated by thirty years the beginning of the public ministry of Jesus. Except for John the Baptist, who will be discussed later, all the other *New Testament* prophets will begin their ministries either during the adulthood of Jesus or after His Resurrection and Ascension. According to Mark:

> *Someone is shouting in the desert, 'Get the road ready for the Lord; make a straight path for him to travel.' (Mark 1:3)*

CHAPTER 3: QUESTIONS FOR REVIEW

1. Why were Mary, Joseph and the infant Jesus required to appear in the Temple forty days after the birth of Jesus?
2. What qualities and virtues of Simeon may account for the special honor he was given by God?
3. What was the nature of the special honor God promised to Simeon?
4. What information about the prophetess Anna is recorded in the Gospel account of St. Luke?
5. What was unique about the way Anna lived her life after the death of her husband?
6. How were the reactions of Simeon and Anna to the Christ Child different? How were they the same?
7. In what ways may the prophetess Anna be viewed as a role model for the women of today?

Chapter Four
JOHN THE BAPTIST

*"John is the one of whom the scripture says, 'God said, I will send
My messenger ahead of you to open the way for you.'"*

The parents of John the Baptist, Elizabeth and Zechariah, can be considered prophets because both received revelations from God about significant future events—and both were able to pass along this special knowledge to others. Surely if they can be called prophets, their son John has an even greater claim to that title as the one designated by God to precede the Messiah and *"prepare His road for Him."* (Luke 1:78)

THE BIRTH OF JOHN

While John is mentioned in all four Gospels, the *Gospel of Luke* is the only Gospel that addresses the birth of John the Baptist, but before delving into his birth, The Gospel makes it clear about his parents that

> *They both lived good lives in God's sight and obeyed fully all the Lord's laws and commands. They had no children because Elizabeth could not have any, and she and Zechariah were both very old. (Luke 1:6-7)*

As mentioned in Chapter 3, John's birth—as well as his name—was first foretold to his father Zechariah, a priest in Jerusalem of the tribe of Levi.

> *One day Zechariah was doing his work as a priest in the Temple, taking his turn in the daily service. According to the custom followed by the priests, he was chosen by lot to burn incense on the altar. So he went into the Temple of the Lord, while the crowd of*

people outside prayed during the hour when the incense was burned. An angel of the Lord appeared to him, standing at the right side of the altar where the incense was burned. When Zechariah saw him, he was alarmed and felt afraid. But the angel said to him, "Don't be afraid, Zechariah! God has heard your prayer, and your wife Elizabeth will bear you a son. You are to name him John. How glad and happy you will be, and how happy many others will be when he is born! He will be a great man in the Lord's sight. He must not drink any wine or strong drink. From his very birth he will be filled with the Holy Spirit, and he will bring back many of the people of Israel to the Lord their God. He will go ahead of the Lord, strong and mighty like the prophet Elijah. He will bring fathers and children together again; he will turn disobedient people back to the way of thinking of the righteous; he will get the Lord's people ready for Him."

Zechariah said to the angel, "How shall I know if this is so? I am an old man, and my wife is old also."

"I am Gabriel," the angel answered. "I stand in the presence of God, Who sent me to speak to you and tell you this good news. But you have not believed my message, which will come true at the right time. Because you have not believed, you will be unable to speak; you will remain silent until the day my promise to you comes true." In the meantime the people were waiting for Zechariah and wondering why he was spending such a long time in the Temple. When he came out, he could not speak to them, and so they knew that he had seen a vision in the Temple. Unable to say a word, he made signs to them with his hands. (Luke 1:8-22)

Scripture does not record how much time elapsed between Gabriel's revelation to Zechariah and Elizabeth's discovery that she was with child, but:

> *Elizabeth became pregnant and did not leave the house for five months. "Now at last the Lord has helped me," she said. "He has taken away my public disgrace!" (Luke 1:24-25)*

The *Gospel of Luke* records that it was in the sixth month of Elizabeth's pregnancy that Gabriel appeared to Mary to announce to her the news that she was to give birth to the Messiah. To allay Mary's doubt and confusion and to extol the power of God, Gabriel revealed to Mary that her aged kinswoman Elizabeth had also become pregnant.

> *Remember your relative Elizabeth. It is said that she cannot have children, but she herself is now six months pregnant, even though she is very old. For there is nothing that God cannot do. (Luke 1:36-37)*

Mary accepted Gabriel's revelation and agreed to serve the Lord, saying:

> *I am the Lord's servant...May it happen to me as you have said." (Luke 1:38)*

Mary decided to visit Elizabeth, who lived in the hillside village of Ein Karem, now a neighborhood on the southwest outskirts of modern Jerusalem. Her motivation for this visit is unclear. She may have required firsthand proof that Gabriel spoke the truth or she may have been motivated by joy, wonder—or the need to commiserate with a kindred spirit about a shared secret. Whatever her reason for seeking Elizabeth might have been, Mary was greeted with great joy and love—a joy and love even shared by John in the womb:

> *When Elizabeth heard Mary's greeting, the baby moved within her. Elizabeth was filled with the Holy Spirit and said in a loud voice, "You are the most blessed of all women, and blessed is the child you will bear! Why should this great thing happen to me, that my Lord's mother comes to visit me? For as soon as I heard your greeting, the baby within me jumped with gladness. How happy are you to believe that the Lord's message to you will come true!" (Luke 1:41-45)*

Was the unborn John offering an *in utero* acknowledgment of Mary's willingness to give birth to the Messiah—and voicing his joy at her decision? Of course, this is a question that one can only answer on the strength of one's faith, but it does offer a great deal of food for thought. The Franciscan Foundation for the Holy Land, which safeguards Christian sites in the Holy Land, recorded on its website that, "John leaped in his mother's womb when he sensed the presence of the Messiah within Mary. If true, this was the first time John would proclaim Jesus as The Anointed One."

One week after John's birth, the time had come for him to be circumcised and named. When Mary announced that the child would be named John, her relatives and neighbors were confused by this break from tradition. It was assumed that the boy would either be named after his father or some other ancestor. When the assemblage then approached Zechariah for confirmation, Zechariah (whose power of speech had been taken away by Gabriel as a penalty for his lack of faith in Gabriel's message) asked for a writing tablet on which he wrote "His name is John." At that moment, Zechariah's ability to speak was restored, and he began to praise God. Zechariah had just suffered many months of muteness, which would have undoubtedly been a humbling experience for him as well as a truly impractical hardship. In his muteness he had to face the lack of faith he displayed when encountering God's angel as well as the magnanimity of the Lord in granting such an honor to his household in the birth of his son.

When asked by those present what they should expect from this infant son, Zechariah delivered what has become known as "Zechariah's Canticle." It is recorded in its entirety in Chapter 3, but Zechariah, in this speech, revealed what he had been told about his son's calling:

> *You, my child, will be called a prophet of the Most High God. You will go ahead of the Lord to prepare His road for Him, to tell His people that they will be saved by having their sins forgiven. (Luke 1:76-77)*

Very little is known about John in the days, months and years following his circumcision and naming—his childhood, adolescence and young adulthood. But we do know that John, like Samuel and Samson before him, took Nazirite vows. In her 2021 monograph "Seven Things You Probably Didn't Know

About John the Baptist," religious author and speaker Karen Scalf Bouchard explained that, "A Nazirite was a person who gave up certain things in order to commune with God in a state of holiness. Nazirites refrained from cutting their hair, drinking alcohol, touching dead bodies, and would sometimes separate themselves from other people in order to eliminate distractions."

In much the same way as we know virtually nothing about the life of Jesus from His Finding in the Temple at about age thirteen to the beginning of His public ministry at the approximate age of thirty, we are equally in the dark about the life of John throughout his formative years. At some point—age unknown—John chose to absent himself from his family and relocate to the desert, where he lived the life of an ascetic. This lifestyle that he chose to adopt is a clear indication of Naziritism. As the *Gospel of Mark* described so John succinctly:

> *John appeared in the desert, baptizing and preaching. "Turn away from your sins and be baptized," he told the people, "and God will forgive your sins." Many people from the province of Judea and the city of Jerusalem went out to hear John. They confessed their sins, and he baptized them in the Jordan River. John wore clothes made of camel's hair, with a leather belt around his waist, and his food was locusts and wild honey. He announced to the people, "The man who will come after me is much greater than I am. I am not good enough even to bend down and untie His sandals. I baptize you with water, but He will baptize you with the Holy Spirit." (Mark 1:4-8)*

Another aspect of John's ministry that remains unclear is the shift in his lifestyle from ascetic to preacher and baptizer. John lived the life of a virtual hermit in the wilderness for an untold period of time as he communed with his thoughts, prayed and prepared himself to take on whatever responsibilities God was entrusting to him. Did he venture out of the desert into Jerusalem to begin to preach and baptize? Did people visit him in the desert out of a sense of curiosity? After all, at some point some Judeans thought John may have been a reincarnated Elijah. How, why and when did John vacate the desert and begin his ministry as a baptist at the River Jordan? Scripture offers no clear insights into these questions, but preacher and author Wayne Jackson, founder of the the journal "The Christian Courier," suggested that, "The citizenry of Jerusalem and all Judea went out unto him as he moved about in the Jordan Valley...His influence was phenomenal. Hundreds, if not thousands, were immersed by him, and his success was solely in the message he proclaimed."

BAPTISM AND TRADITION

John's use of the ritual of baptism as a symbol of repentance for one's sins and desire to return to a state of personal purity is a reflection of the longstanding Jewish custom of the *mikveh*, or ritual bath, as outlined in chapter 15 of the *Book of Leviticus*. Observant Jews used immersion in the mikveh to achieve ritual purity if they were thought to have become defiled from a number of different sources (i.e. sexual activity, menstruation, skin conditions, contact with a corpse or grave, etc.) or at the beginning of a new commitment to God. Moses also presided over a baptism ritual at Mount Sinai—where the Israelites were sprinkled with blood rather than water—as a sign of commitment to Yahweh and His covenant:

> *Then he [Moses] took the book of the covenant, in which the Lord's commands were written, and read it aloud to the people. They said, "We will obey the Lord and do everything that He has commanded."*
>
> *Then Moses took the blood in the bowls and threw it on the people. He said, "This is the blood that seals the covenant which the Lord made with you when He gave all these commands." (Exodus 24:7-8)*

Much of John's life and ministry hearkens back to Old Testament traditions and values, such that he is often referred to as the last great prophet of the *Old* Testament (despite the fact that he appears only in the *New* Testament.) As a member of the priestly tribe of Israel through both of his parents, tradition would have dictated that John serve the people of Judea as a *kohen*, a priest—but God, of course, had other plans for him, and his parents were aware of these plans virtually from his conception. John's use of the ritual of baptism also reflects Jewish traditions going all the way back to Moses. And, as Dr. Jirair Tashjian, a professor of New Testament Studies at Southern Nazarene University in Oklahoma, pointed out in 2018, "Since Elijah was taken up to heaven in a whirlwind, the Jews believed that someday he would come back. *Malachi*, the last canonical book of the Old Testament, promises that God will send Elijah to warn people before the day of judgment.

People who saw and heard John were reminded that he may very well be the promised Elijah."

It is unknown whether or not John and Jesus ever met one another face-to-face before John baptized Jesus in the River Jordan at the advent of Jesus' public ministry. Despite the fact that they were members of the same extended family, it was not necessarily true that they spent time together during their formative years. As the Sisters of St. John the Baptist pointed out on their American Provincial website, "Scripture is silent about John until it records his appearance in the Judean desert where he lived as a hermit until about A.D. 27. When he was thirty, he began to preach on the banks of the Jordan against the evils of the times."

JOHN'S MISSION AND MESSAGE

John's primary role in salvation history was to prepare the people of Judea for the imminent arrival of the Messiah, and the ritual of baptism that he administered was center stage in this preparation. Theologians see this truth of John's role foreshadowed in the words of both Isaiah and Malachi centuries before John's birth. Isaiah wrote:

> *A voice cries out, "Prepare in the wilderness a road for the Lord! Clear the way in the desert for our God! Fill every valley; level every mountain. The hills will become a plain, and the rough country will be made smooth. Then the glory of the Lord will be revealed, and all mankind will see it. The Lord Himself has promised this." (Isaiah 40:3-5)*

Malachi also prophesied:

The Lord Almighty answers, "I will send My messenger to prepare the way for Me. Then the Lord you are looking for will suddenly come to His Temple. The messenger you long to see will come and proclaim My covenant." (Malachi 3:1)

And while John's mission was primarily one of preparation, contained within this ministry can be found several distinct yet related messages, messages John delivered throughout the territory around the Jordan River, and preached over and over again: (1) the necessity of repentance for one's sins, (2) the coming of the Day of Judgment, (3) the arrival of Jesus as the Messiah of God.

REPENTANCE FOR ONE'S SINS IS NECESSARY

Wayne Jackson, the founder of ChristianCourier.com, explained in his 2022 monograph "Who was John the Baptist?" that "the Palestine in which the prophet's ministry was launched was firmly in the grip of a grossly pagan force, the Roman Empire….Moral corruption had made deep inroads into Judaism as well. John's message of repentance entailed a deep consciousness of offense to God within the sinner's heart, with a required reformation of life." Hence, John's message reverberated throughout the desert with words such as:

Turn away from your sins and be baptized, and God will forgive your sins. (Luke 3:3)

> *Turn away from your sins...because the Kingdom of heaven is near. (Matthew 3:2)*

THE DAY OF JUDGMENT IS COMING

For John, the ritual of baptism was only the beginning of authentic and necessary repentance and reformation. While baptism *was* a public act of contrition and conviction, he required concrete and ongoing alterations in individual behavior as well.

> *Crowds of people came out to John to be baptized by Him. "You snakes!" he said to them. "Who told you that you could escape from the punishment God is about to send? Do those things that show that you have turned from your sins. And don't start saying among yourselves that Abraham is your ancestor. I tell you that God can take these rocks and make descendants for Abraham! The ax is ready to cut down the trees at the roots; every tree that does not bear good fruit will be cut down and thrown into the fire."*
>
> *The people asked him, "What are we to do, then?" He answered, "Whoever has two shirts must give one to the man who has none, and whoever has food must share it."*
>
> *Some tax collectors came to be baptized, and they asked him, "Teacher, what are we to do?" "Don't collect more than is legal," he told them.*
>
> *Some soldiers also asked him, "What about us? What are we to do?" He said to them, "Don't take money from anyone by force or accuse anyone falsely. Be content with your pay." (Luke 3:7-14)*

THE MESSIAH OF GOD HAS ARRIVED

Throughout his public ministry John never lost sight of the fact that his role was to prepare the people of Judea for the imminent arrival of the Messiah. He made it abundantly clear that:

> *I baptize you with water to show that you have repented, but the One Who will come after me will baptize you with the Holy Spirit and fire. He is much greater than I am, and I am not good enough even to carry His sandals. He has His winnowing shovel with Him to thresh out all the grain. He will gather His wheat into His barn, but He will burn the chaff in a fire that never goes out. (Matthew 3:11-12)*

And when John laid eyes on Jesus, he specifically identified Him as the Messiah for Whose coming he was preparing the people:

> *John saw Jesus coming to him, and said, "There is the Lamb of God, Who takes away the sin of the world. This is the One I was talking about when I said, 'A man is coming after me, but He is greater than I am, because He existed before I was born.' I did not know Who He would be, but I came baptizing with water in order to make Him known to the people of Israel." (John 1:29-31)*

> *And John gave this testimony: "I saw the Spirit come down like a dove from heaven and stay on Him. I still did not know that He was the One, but God, Who sent me to baptize with water, had said to me, 'You will see the Spirit come down and stay on a man; He is the One Who baptizes with the Holy Spirit.' I have seen it... and I tell you that He is the Son of God." (John 1:32-34)*

In the above citations from the *Gospel of John*, John the Baptist claims not to have known the identity of the Messiah until his baptism of Jesus in the River Jordan. John's late notice of the identity of the Messiah is also seemingly echoed in the earlier *Gospel of Matthew*:

> *At that time Jesus arrived from Galilee and came to John at the Jordan to be baptized by him. But John tried to make Him change His mind. "I ought to be baptized by You," John said, "and yet You have come to me!"*
>
> *But Jesus answered him, "Let it be so for now. For in this way we shall do all that God requires." So John agreed.*
>
> *As soon as Jesus was baptized, He came up out of the water. Then heaven was opened to Him, and He saw the Spirit of God coming down like a dove and lighting on Him. Then a voice said from heaven, "This is My own dear Son, with Whom I am pleased." (Matthew 3:13-17)*

It's unclear in Matthew's account exactly when John recognized Jesus as the Messiah, but he seems to be aware of Jesus' identity before the arrival of the dove and the voice from heaven. This, of course, begs the questions: what did John know about the identity of the Messiah—and when did he know it?—questions never to have definitive answers.

JOHN'S IMPRISONMENT AND DEATH

It should be noted that the imprisonment and death of John the Baptist was really not directly attributable to his preaching about repentance, the Day of Judgment or the Messiahship of Jesus. It was his moral criticism of King Herod Antipas that ultimately led to his execution. As prolific Christian author Debbie McDaniel explained in her 2021 "iBelieve" monograph "Six Powerful Truths from the Life of John the Baptist That Offer Hope for Today," it was John's courage and devotion to the truth that sealed his fate. "John was not afraid of the religious or political leaders of his day. He saw beyond their exterior into the deeper heart. He spoke the truth with clarity and passion, he didn't live to people-please, simply to preach the need for forgiveness of sin… He spoke the hard truth to Herod, one of the four rulers over Palestine. When Herod had taken Herodias, his brother Philip's wife, to become his own, John had said to him, *'It is not lawful for you to have her.' (Matthew 14:4)* It had bothered Herod so much that he had John imprisoned; he wanted to kill him but was afraid of the people because so many considered him to be a great prophet. But at his birthday celebration, in response to a promise he had given to the daughter of Herodias [Salome], John's life was tragically ended. *'Prompted by her mother, she said, 'Give me here on a platter the head of John the Baptist'." (Matthew 14:8)*

Herod's attitude toward John has been the subject of lively debate. While it is certainly true that Herod authorized his beheading at the request of Herodias' daughter Salome (at Herodias' intervention), it is not necessarily true that it was the result of his own volition.

> *Herodias held a grudge against John and wanted to kill him, but she could not because of Herod. Herod was afraid of John because*

> *he knew that John was a good and holy man, and so he kept him safe. He liked to listen to him, even though he became greatly disturbed every time he heard him. (Mark 6:19-20)*

After young Salome, with whom it is believed Herod was quite smitten, danced—most likely erotically—at his birthday celebration, he wanted to show his appreciation with a magnanimous gesture.

> *So the king said to the girl, "What would you like to have? I will give you anything you want." With many vows he said to her, "I swear that I will give you anything you ask for, even as much as half my kingdom!" (Mark 6:22-23)*

After consulting with her mother Herodias, Salome demanded the head of John the Baptist on a platter, which was certainly not a request anticipated or supported by Herod. But he had been successfully manipulated by Herodias in such a way that he would "lose face" if he refused the request.

> *This made the king very sad, but he could not refuse her because of the vows he had made in front of all his guests. So he sent off a guard at once with orders to bring John's head. The guard left, went to the prison, and cut John's head off; then he brought it on a plate and gave it to the girl, who gave it to her mother. When John's disciples heard about this, they came and got his body, and buried it. (Mark 6:26-29)*

To this day, twenty centuries later, Karen Scalf Bouchard has pointed out that "John the Baptist's head is considered a relic by many. So much so that four different locations are said to provide the final resting place for the head...the first is the Umayyad Mosque in Damascus, Syria. Similarly, the Residenz Museum in Munich, Germany claims to have John's head among other relics collected by Duke Wilhelm V in the sixth century. And if you happen to visit Rome, you may come across his alleged skull at the Church of San Silvestro in Capite. Finally, the 13th century cathedral in Amiens, France was built for the sole purpose of housing John's head, supposedly... carried from Constantinople in 1206."

THE FINAL DOUBT AND VINDICATION

Before John's untimely death, while imprisoned by Herod, word of the miracles of Jesus began to spread throughout the countryside, most recently about Jesus' healing of the Roman officer's servant and His raising from death the son of the widow in Nain. The questions of the extent of John's knowledge with regard to the purpose of his own ministry as well as the depth of his relationship with his kinsman Jesus have already been raised, but these questions surfaced one last time during John's imprisonment. Exactly what did he know about Jesus?

> When John's disciples told him about all these things [the miracles of Jesus], *he called two of them and sent them to the Lord to ask Him, "Are You the One John said was going to come, or should we expect someone else?...At that very time Jesus healed many people from their sicknesses, diseases and evil spirits, and gave sight to many blind people. He answered John's messengers, "Go*

> back and tell John what you have seen and heard: the blind can see, the lame can walk, those who suffer from dreaded skin diseases are made clean, the deaf can hear, the dead are raised to life, and the Good News is preached to the poor. How happy are those who have no doubts about Me!" (Luke 7:18-23)

John's decision to ask several of his followers to approach and question Jesus is not a sign of a weakened faith as much as it was a validation of his own ministry and a search for confirmation that his preaching and baptisms were on the right track. But the arrival of these messengers from John afforded Jesus with an opportunity to speak about John and the pivotal role he had been asked to play in the unfolding of God's plan of salvation.

> Jesus began to speak about him [John] to the crowds: "When you went out to John into the desert, what did you expect to see? A blade of grass bending in the wind? What did you go out to see? A man dressed up in fancy clothes? People who dress like that and live in luxury are found in palaces! Tell Me, what did you go out to see? A prophet? Yes indeed, but you saw much more than a prophet. For John is the one of whom the scripture says, 'God said, I will send My messenger ahead of You to open the way for You.' I tell you," Jesus added, "John is greater than any man who has ever lived. But he who is least in the Kingdom of God is greater than John." (Luke 7:24-28)

Perhaps no greater words of praise have ever been uttered about a human being at any point in human history, and coming from Jesus Himself, the words "John is greater than any man who has ever lived" resound with unsurpassed clarity and strength. And if there were any doubt whatsoever about John's status as a prophet of God, these words of Jesus dispelled those doubts with absolute certitude.

And Wayne Jackson put these words in an historical context when he concluded, "The fact that the birth of Christianity was such a resounding phenomenon, impacting the ancient world tremendously, and echoing marvelously across the centuries, is, in some measure, a commentary on how well John accomplished his mission."

CHAPTER 4: QUESTIONS FOR REVIEW

1. What was unusual about the manner in which Zechariah discovered he would have a son?
2. How and why was Zechariah punished by Gabriel?
3. What is meant by the term "Nazirite" that is used to describe John?
4. Why did John employ the ritual of baptism as a central aspect of his ministry?
5. What is the connection between John and the *Old Testament* prophet Elijah?
6. Did John and Jesus have a close relationship growing up as relatives?
7. What was the primary mission entrusted by God to John the Baptist?
8. What are the 3 major messages that John hoped to convey to the people of Israel?
9. How did John describe Jesus to the people to whom he preached?
10. What was the nature of the criticism John directed at Herod? How did this lead to his death?

Chapter Five
BARNABAS

*"Barnabas was a good man, full of the Holy Spirit and faith,
And many people were brought to the Lord"*

In today's world, the term "socialism" has mixed connotations. For some (older people, mostly!), it hearkens back to the Union of Soviet Socialist Republics, the Cold War, atheistic dictatorship, the "Red Menace" or "Red Scare" and totalitarianism. For others (usually the younger crowd), it conjures images of generosity, the sharing of wealth, assets and personal belongings, and a fervent desire to reach out in service to the underprivileged. Perhaps both connotations have some validity. But it is this second understanding of socialism—the kinder, gentler, more altruistic interpretation—that brings us to Barnabas.

Chapter 4 of the *Acts of the Apostles* introduces us to the mindset and value system of the infant community of believers as the early Church began to flourish and grow:

> *The group of believers was one in mind and heart. No one said that any of his belongings was his own, but they all shared with one another everything they had. With great power the apostles gave witness to the resurrection of the Lord Jesus, and God poured rich blessings on them all. There was no one in the group who was in need. Those who owned fields and houses would sell them, bring the money received from the sale, and turn it over to the apostles; and the money was distributed to each one according to his need. (Acts 4:32-35)*

It is with this peek into the early Church that we are first introduced to Barnabas:

> *And so it was that Joseph, a Levite born in Cyprus, whom the apostles called Barnabas (which means "one who encourages"), sold a field he owned, brought the money, and turned it over to the apostles. (Acts 4:36-37)*

ENCOURAGEMENT THROUGH WORDS AND FUNDING

Much has been written—and will be discussed further in this chapter—about the time Barnabas spent with St. Paul on his missionary journeys to various locations throughout the Mediterranean world, but the first time Scripture introduces Barnabas, it is to extol his generosity of spirit and offer a few brief insights into his background and personality. In his monograph entitled "Barnabas: 43 Facts and Lessons from the Life of a Disciple," Dr. Dan Lioy of the South African Theological Seminary and Institute of Lutheran Theology offered some interesting insights into Joseph, called Barnabas. Dr Lioy suggests that the nickname "Barnabas," associated with encouragement, demonstrates a capacity for sensitivity and empathy in the comforting of those facing any sort of affliction or crisis. The fact that Barnabas was a Levite, a sanctuary official with various duties in the Temple, shows his familiarity with Mosaic Law and religious customs and rituals. As a resident of Cyprus, Barnabas, in all probability, spoke Greek and was familiar with Greek culture and its customs and traditions.

Dr. Lioy also theorized that since Levites were usually supported financially by funds generated through the Temple system, and Barnabas was able and willing to sell real estate holdings, he was probably a landowner on Cyprus—but was not a "hoarder" for whom material wealth was a top priority. His willingness to sell his land and turn its proceeds over to the apostles was indicative of that.

PARTNERSHIP WITH PAUL

When one reads the *New Testament* and encounters Barnabas, it is, more often than not, in tandem with his companion, and perhaps mentor, Paul. Barnabas' adventures are discussed throughout the *Acts of the Apostles* as well as in several of the Pauline epistles, including *1st Corinthians, Galatians* and *Colossians*. After Barnabas' material and financial generosity is regaled in *Acts 4*, his unwavering support of Saul, in the face of a great deal of suspicion on the part of the apostles, shows an equal measure of emotional generosity. In Chapter 9, he presents and defends Paul as a recent and deeply committed convert:

> *Then Barnabas came to his [Saul's] help and took him to the apostles. He explained to them how Saul had seen the Lord on the road and that the Lord had spoken to him. He also told them how boldly Saul had preached in the name of Jesus in Damascus. And so Saul stayed with them and went all over Jerusalem, preaching boldly in the name of the Lord. (Acts 9:27-28)*

Clearly, the words of Barnabas made a difference, as the apostles embraced Saul as one of their own and granted him a great deal of freedom in spreading the word of the risen Christ to others—and especially to the Gentile (non-Jewish) community. It is obvious that the opinion of Barnabas was held in very high regard for the apostles and their comrades to reverse their assessment of Saul so quickly and completely.

As some members of the early church, inspired by Peter, began to spread the word of the risen Lord to non-Jews, Barnabas was sent to Antioch to continue this evangelization. Many Gentiles in Antioch had already embraced faith in the risen Jesus, and Barnabas, upon his arrival, was overjoyed to see this.

> *He was glad and urged them all to be faithful and true to the Lord with all their hearts. Barnabas was a good man, full of the Holy Spirit and faith, and many people were brought to the Lord. (Acts 11:23-24)*

Barnabas also had a positive influence on the people of Antioch through his faith and example, and then left Antioch to travel to Tarsus, Saul's hometown, to find him. They returned together to Antioch and remained there for a year, meeting the people and teaching them, until they were called to return to Jerusalem with funds that were earmarked to help those in need after a different prophet (Agabus) had predicted a severe upcoming famine. Upon the completion of their mission, Barnabas and Saul returned to Antioch yet again. It was at Antioch that the followers of Jesus were first called "Christians."

If a prophet is an individual who has been called by God to deliver a message or complete a mission, then it is at this juncture that Barnabas can be labeled a "prophet." Even though Scripture has already described Barnabas as being *"a good man, full of the Holy Spirit..." (Acts 11:24* above), it is at this moment—during his return to Antioch—that Barnabas (along with Saul) is referred to in Scripture as a "prophet" for the first time—and given a direct assignment from God:

> *In the church at Antioch there were some prophets and teachers: Barnabas, Simeon (called the Black), Lucius (from Cyrene), Manaen (who had been brought up with Governor Herod) and Saul. While they were serving the Lord and fasting, the Holy Spirit said to them, 'Set apart for Me Barnabas and Saul, to do the work to which I have called them.' (Acts 13:1-2)*

Thus Scripture verifies Barnabas as a person chosen by God to deliver His message—the usual definition of a prophet. Barnabas and Saul sailed from the Syrian port city of Seleucia to the island of Cyprus, where they crossed the island from east to west, from the city of Salamis to Paphos. On this journey, Saul and Barnabas were accompanied by Barnabas' cousin John Mark (called at other times either just "John" or "Mark.") After leaving Cyprus, they sailed from Paphos northwest to Perga, a city in Pamphylia, and then further north to Antioch in Pisidia. John Mark left them in Perga to return to Jerusalem. [Please note: there are two ancient cities named Antioch—one in Syria and the other in Pisidia.]

At Antioch in Pisidia, Barnabas and Saul made many converts among Jews and Gentiles alike, but also faced opposition to their teachings to such an extent that they were forced to leave. They traveled southeast to the city of Iconium, where they encountered much of the same—conversion of some and hostility from others. From Iconium they moved on to Lystra, where a miracle performed by Saul (who we will now call Paul) led the local inhabitants to treat them as if they were gods. Paul and Barnabas protested this treatment and tried to re-focus the attention of the Lystra citizens on God. However, hostile Jews from Pisidia and Iconium arrived on the scene, turned the Lystrans away from Paul and Barnabas, and forced the two to move on to the town of Derbe. As Jesus once told His disciples:

> If some home or town will not welcome you or listen to you, then leave that place and shake the dust off your feet. (Matthew 10:14)

Paul and Barnabas preached successfully in Derbe and converted many to faith in Jesus. But after a time their missionary travels took them back to Lystra, Iconium and Antioch, Pisidia, and later to Perga and Attalia in Pamphylia. In these places they tried to strengthen and support the faith of the believers, before they returned once again to Antioch, where a controversy that required resolution began to erupt. Other unnamed disciples had also arrived in Antioch from Judea and announced that the Antiochian converts had to be circumcised under the Law of Moses—a requirement completely opposed by Paul and Barnabas, and a requirement that had not been authorized by the infant church's leadership —the Apostles and elders—in Jerusalem.

In Paul's *Epistle to the Galatians*, he discusses a moment in Antioch when both Peter and Barnabas wrongly deferred to these religious legalists by refusing to eat with Gentiles in their presence after having previously done so openly:

> *When Peter came to Antioch, I opposed him in public, because he was clearly wrong. Before some men who had been sent by James arrived there, Peter had been eating with the Gentile brothers. But after these men arrived, he drew back and would not eat with the Gentiles, because he was afraid of those who were in favor of circumcising them. The other Jewish brothers also started acting like cowards along with Peter, and even Barnabas was swept along by their cowardly action. (Galatians 2:11-13)*

THE COUNCIL AT JERUSALEM

Paul rebuked Peter for his inconsistency, and thus, a summit was scheduled in Jerusalem to resolve this issue. The church summit gave Barnabas and Paul an opportunity to present to the assembled leadership the miracles and conversions that their ministry to the Gentiles had experienced without the requirement of circumcision as a prerequisite. Both Peter and James agreed that circumcision of the Gentile converts should not be required, with James suggesting:

> *We should not trouble the Gentiles who are turning to God. Instead, we should write a letter telling them not to eat any food that is ritually unclean because it has been offered to idols, to keep themselves from sexual immorality, and not to eat any animal that has been strangled, or any blood. (Acts 15:19-20)*

Barnabas and Paul, along with Judas (called Barsabbas) and Silas, were sent back to Antioch to deliver both a verbal and written message that circumcision would not be required—

which was cause for elation among the Gentile converts—and they remained there for a time.

Paul suggested to Barnabas that it would be a worthwhile venture to return to the other towns where they had preached to check on the seeds they had planted, but when Barnabas wished to include his cousin John Mark, an argument ensued. Paul did not want to include him because John Mark had left them on their previous missionary trip to return to Jerusalem—his reason for leaving never coming to light. This argument led to a separation: Barnabas took John Mark to sail to Cyprus while Paul took Silas on a journey through Syria and Cilicia. The *Acts of the Apostles* offers no further information about Barnabas and his journey with John Mark, nor does it mention Barnabas again.

It's possible that the story of the prophetic ministry of Barnabas ends here but, then again, perhaps there is still a little bit more. Outside of the *Acts of the Apostles* and Paul's *Letter to the Galatians*, several other writings concerning Barnabas have come to light. Their authenticity and accuracy are both called into question, but it is appropriate to mention them nevertheless.

BARNABAS' ACTS, EPISTLE AND GOSPEL?

Pseudepigrapha is a word that's used to describe religious writings of unknown or misnamed authors written generally between the years 300 BCE and 300 CE—non-canonical texts not included in either the *Old* or *New Testaments*. Several of these texts have been affiliated with Barnabas—either as its author or its subject, but modern Biblical scholars refute the connection. The first of these pseudepigraphal works is called the *Epistle of Barnabas*, and was supposedly composed by the Cypriot apostle between 70 and 132 CE. According to Reverend Maxwell Staniforth, who translated the text, important Church Fathers such as Clement of Alexandria and Jerome attributed the work to Barnabas while Eusebius thought it not to be inspired.

In a nutshell, according to Staniforth, the author of the *Epistle of Barnabas* denies any connection whatsoever between Judaism and the Gospel—that the rituals of the Mosaic Law, which were meant by God to be spiritual "pointers" to Jesus, were taken literally by Jews under the inspiration of an evil angel to be "sufficient ends unto themselves." The result of this misguided interpretation of the Law of Moses is that the Covenant between God and His Chosen People extends to the followers of Christ rather than the Jews. Staniforth concludes that the "real" Barnabas, who was a Levite, would never have, could never have connected the Law of Moses with machinations of an evil angel, or demon.

The *Acts of Barnabas* is another pseudepigraphal work that was purportedly written by Barnabas' cousin John Mark and discusses the details of their missionary trip to Cyprus after they separated from Paul. The North American Society for the Study of Apocryphal Christian Literature (NASSCAL) summarized this text as it pertains to Barnabas in describing several of his accomplishments—such as converting several Greek sailors to the faith, healing the sick by touching them with a copy of the *Gospel of Matthew*, razing an idolatrous temple, and establishing churches and teaching converts in Salamis. Barnabas was supposedly attacked by a band of hostile Judeans who martyred Barnabas by setting him on fire. John Mark managed to save and bury the remains of Barnabas in a cave on Cyprus, eventually escaping to Alexandria, Egypt where he continued to preach and baptize.

Biblical scholars trace the composition of the *Acts of Barnabas* to the fifth century CE, where its composition was thought to be an attempt to show a direct link of apostolic succession through Barnabas to the church in Cyprus, so authorship of the text by John Mark is thought to be highly unlikely.

The last extratestamental work attributed to Barnabas is the *Gospel of Barnabas*, which was apparently in circulation in the first and second centuries CE, and was widely quoted by Church Father Irenaeus in the second century. Very little is really known of this text, but it is thought that it may have been altered and re-materialized in the late sixteenth century, written in Italian and in Spanish. These possibly redacted texts are also of questionable authorship due to the relative recency of their discovery, language and the strong Islamic influence upon them. According to the website CompellingTruth.org, "Muslim influence is seen throughout the text. The *shahadah* prayer (an Islamic creedal statement) is mentioned directly (chapter 39). Muhammad is noted by name. The Trinity is spoken against (a major Muslim criticism of Christianity), and Jesus is noted as a prophet rather than the Messiah or Son of God, consistent with Muslim teachings." The website goes on to relate that "Historical inaccuracies have been found within the *Gospel of Barnabas*. For example, it teaches Jesus was born in the time of Pilate (though Pilate became leader in AD 26), that Adam and Eve ate an apple as the forbidden fruit (the fruit is unspecified in the Bible), and that Jesus sailed across the Sea of Galilee to Nazareth (though Nazareth is not a coastal town)."

It is clear that Barnabas, though not one of the original twelve Apostles, made a significant contribution to the development and growth of the early Church, especially as it spread throughout the Gentile population of the Mediterranean world. As David Sanford of the Christian Leadership Alliance concluded, "The early Church wouldn't have grown as fast, and half of the *New Testament* wouldn't have been written, without Barnabas' encouragement...John Mark could have disappeared from history, but Barnabas...encourages him and enlists him back into the Lord's service. Later, tradition says [John] Mark has the courage to write the Gospel that bears his name. Saul would never have become Paul without spending several years apprenticing under Barnabas. Later, Paul wrote more than a dozen letters accepted by the Apostles as part of God's inspired Word. Few Christians have contributed more to the advancement of the Church than Barnabas."

CHAPTER 5: QUESTIONS FOR REVIEW

1. What qualities do Scripture and Biblical scholars attribute to Barnabas about his personality and value system?
2. In what ways is Paul in the debt of Barnabas?
3. In what cities and lands did Barnabas and Paul preach about the risen Christ?
4. Were the missionary journeys of Barnabas and Paul successful? Explain why or why not.
5. Why did Barnabas and Paul decide to separate?
6. Why is it thought that the various writings ascribed to Barnabas *(Acts, Epistle* and *Gospel)* may have been written by other authors?

Chapter Six
SIMEON NIGER, LUCIUS, AND MANAEN

"In the church at Antioch there were some prophets and teachers...
Simeon (called the Black), Lucius (from Cyrene), Manaen..."

The citation from *Acts* that opens this chapter contains all the information about these three prophets that the *New Testament* has to offer. Clearly, it's not much to go on. So to "flush out" more information about these prophets, it becomes necessary to seek alternative sources of information and/or to draw some deductive conclusions based on the limited data that is available.

Theologian and author Sam O'Neal pointed out that "There are literally thousands of people mentioned in the Bible. Many of these individuals are well-known and have been studied throughout history because they played major roles in the events recorded throughout Scripture. Prominent Biblical characters include people such as Moses, King David, the apostle Paul, and so on. But most of the people mentioned in the Bible are buried a little deeper within the pages, people whose names may not be recognized right away."

"A man named Simeon, who was also called Niger, is one of these characters. Outside of some dedicated *New Testament* scholars, very few people have heard of him or know about his story. And yet his presence in the New Testament may signal some important facts about the early church of the *New Testament*, facts that point to some surprising implications."

SIMEON THE NIGER

According to Lutheran Pastor Karl Anderson, "Among the noted prophets and teachers of the church in Antioch was a man named Simeon, who was called Niger. Niger is not a name, but the Latin word for black. Obviously, Simeon was a black man. To describe a man as part of his name is not unusual in the *New Testament*. James and John were the "Sons of Thunder." Thomas is further nicknamed as "the Twin." Simon is better known as Peter, which means "rock." And there was Simon the Zealot and Matthew the Tax Collector. So it is generally concluded that Simeon was called Niger because he was black."

Sam O'Neal offered a reminder that, "By the time we get to *Acts 13* [where Simeon is mentioned], the Church has already experienced a powerful wave of persecution from both Jewish and Roman authorities. More importantly, the Church leaders had begun discussing whether Gentiles (non-Jewish people) should be told about the gospel message and included within the Church...He [Simeon] is presumed to be an African Gentile who had transplanted to Antioch and met with Jesus."

The presence of Simeon in the Christian community at Antioch does not only demonstrate the omniracial composition of the early Church, but its inclusion of Simeon as a leader of the Antioch Church community as both a prophet and teacher demonstrates him to be authoritative and highly regarded, such that:

> Simeon [with Lucius and Manaen]...fasted and prayed, placed their hands on them [Barnabas and Saul], and sent them off. (Acts 13:2)

The position of prominence held by Simeon demonstrates not only a Christian community composed of members of different races, but also shows a Church in which leadership is not based on ethnic or racial considerations. Quite refreshing in an age where slavery and ethnic strife were endemic. It was Simeon, along with Lucius and Manaen, who authorized a missionary trip for Barnabas and Saul, and blessed them as they commenced their journey.

Pastor David Kosobucki of Horizon Central Christian Fellowship in Indianapolis offered an interesting hypothesis that future biblical historians may very well corroborate. He suggested that Simeon Niger, leader of the Antioch Christian community, and Simon of Cyrene, who helped Jesus carry His cross to Calvary, may very well be one and the same person. While the facts that he presented are merely speculative, they nevertheless posit an interesting connection on several different levels.

On his personal website, Pastor Kosobucki first recalls that "Simeon and Simon are alternative spellings of the same name." Second, he mentions that Simeon is a Jewish name and that Niger, meaning black, was added to his name because of his dark-skinned appearance. He mentions that "There are and have long been dark-skinned Jews" and that "They are a minority...but they mainly come from Africa." Since nowhere in Scripture is it mentioned where Simeon Niger hails from, and the Christian community in Antioch "was founded by men from Cyprus and Cyrene," these facts could conceivably connect Simeon with the Simon of Cyrene who came to Christ's aid on the road to Calvary. It would also indicate that Simeon did not embrace faith in Christ as a result of proselytization after Christ's Ascension, but rather through a personal encounter with Jesus before His Crucifixion.

It was the Evangelists Matthew, Mark and Luke who recorded the encounter between Simon of Cyrene and Jesus, but it is only Mark who mentioned that

> *Simon was from Cyrene and was the father of Alexander and Rufus. (Mark 15:21)*

This innocuous bit of information about Simon's sons may offer yet another connection—albeit, perhaps, a weak one—between Simeon and Simon. Mark (also known as John Mark, as mentioned in the previous chapter), Simeon, Saul/Paul and Barnabas were all well-acquainted with one another through the Antioch community. Both Mark and Paul directed their writings (the *Gospel of Mark* and Paul's *Epistle to the Romans*) to a largely Roman audience, and it is in Paul's epistle that he mentions Rufus [the son of Simon?] by name:

> *I send greetings to Rufus, that outstanding worker in the Lord's service, and to his mother, who has always treated me like a son. (Romans 16:13)*

It is plausible, then, in the opinion of Pastor Kosobucki that "Simon of Cyrene became a believer in Jesus Christ, and his sons were well-known in the early church. He later traveled to Antioch and helped get the church there started. His wife and sons were with him. In Antioch he received the nickname Niger, 'the black guy,' for being a dark-skinned Jew....He was later joined in Antioch by Paul (then Saul of Tarsus) and, later yet, John Mark, who both got to know and love him, his wife and sons. Years later, after Simon's/Niger's death, his wife and son Rufus were living in Rome. They were prominent in the church there, in part because of the unique role Simon played in the Gospel story. Writing to a Roman audience, Mark mentions Rufus and Alexander, because he and the Roman church knew them personally. Paul, writing [also] to the Romans, greets Rufus and his mom for the same reason."

LUCIUS OF CYRENE

Lucius is yet another prophet about whom little is written but much is conjectured. Described as a "Cyrenian," he is thought to have either emigrated from Cyrene, a city in what is now eastern Libya or from the greater Roman African province of Creta at Cyrenaica, which was one of the centers of Judaism after the Roman Diaspora of 70 CE that scattered the Jewish population from Judea. Whether Lucius originally hailed from Cyrene—and is of African heritage—and whether he was black—is unknown. But it is generally assumed that Lucius migrated from Africa to Antioch, where he is considered to be one of the founders of the Christian church in that city.

It is possible, though historically unsubstantiated, that Lucius may have been present at the stoning of St. Stephen, the first Christian martyr, at the hands of the Jewish High Council, the Sanhedrin:

> *Some of the believers who were scattered by the persecution which took place when Stephen was killed went as far as Phoenicia, Cyprus and Antioch, telling the message to Jews only. But other believers, men from Cyprus and Cyrene, went to Antioch and proclaimed the message to Gentiles also, telling them the Good News about the Lord Jesus. The Lord's power was with them, and a great number of people believed and turned to the Lord. (Acts 11:19-21)*

While this passage certainly does not mention Lucius by name, it is conceivable that he was among the Jews from Cyrene who traveled to Antioch and took it upon themselves to preach not only to Jews, but to Gentiles as well, helping to establish a Christian community there.

As is often the case when different individuals from the same time period have similar names, it has also been postulated that Lucius of Cyrene may be one and the same as the evangelist Luke, in much the same way that Simeon Niger is sometimes—accurately or inaccurately—equated with Simon the Cyrene, who aided Jesus on the road to Calvary. However, this correlation is largely rejected by Biblical historians, who find no evidence to support the idea that the evangelist Luke came from North Africa, but rather was native to Syria, perhaps even to Antioch.

While Lucius' background may be the subject of ongoing debate and conjecture, it is universally accepted that Lucius was an important leader in the Christian church at Antioch— perhaps even a founder of that community. *Acts* defines him as a prophet and teacher and credits him (along with Simeon and

Manaen) as authorizing the first missionary journey of Barnabas and Saul/Paul as well as blessing them with the laying on of hands.

Methodist theologian Thomas C. Oden lists Lucius as the first bishop of Cyrene, so it is clear that his impact on the early church was both extensive and protracted. Like so many of the other *New Testament* prophets whose names are largely unrecognized and uncelebrated, Lucius made a real contribution that should not be forgotten.

MANAEN

Manaen rounds out the trio of prophet/teachers mentioned in *Acts 13*, but his life and entry into the Christian community took a turn unlike the personal stories of Simeon Niger and Lucius the Cyrene. To appreciate the uniqueness of Manaen's circumstances, it is necessary to take a brief side trip into the Judean history immediately preceding Manaen's birth. The story begins with King Herod the Great.

Herod was the puppet monarch of Judea, installed by the Romans in 37 BCE. His tenure was a controversial one, much debated by historians. Apologists of Herod extolled his massive construction campaigns at the Second Temple and Temple Mount, the port at Caesarea Maritima and the fortresses at Masada and Herodium, while detractors criticized his outrageous expenditures, the impoverishment of many of his people, and the disdain with which he was held by Jews and Gentiles alike.

It has been speculated that Herod would stop at nothing to retain power—including the murder of political enemies and family members alike, including his wife Mariamne and several sons and in-laws. It has also been posited that he ordered the "Slaughter of the Innocents"—the killing of all Jewish male infants under the age of two in Bethlehem to prevent his succession or overthrow by a future, long-awaited Messiah. Historians, frankly, question the validity of the accusation just as they question the existence of the three Magi from Persia whose astronomical projections about a bright, rogue star led to the horrific decree.

Upon the death of Herod the Great in 4 or 5 BCE, his kingdom was divided into four quadrants to be ruled by three of his sons, specifically Archelaus, Herod Antipas, Philip and his sister, Salome I. It is with these relatives of Herod the Great—and especially Herod Antipas—that the story of Manaen takes root. Manaen is described as being a *syntrophos* of Herod Antipas— this Greek word is translated in different places as either "foster brother" or "lifelong friend." In either event, the word describes a very close relationship between Manaen and Herod Antipas in which they spent a great deal of time together and shared many common experiences. Little is known about how this relationship came into being and how the young Manaen found himself in the palace of Herod. Perhaps it doesn't really matter. What is known is that Herod Antipas grew up in the household of a father who was quite ruthless, ambitious, immoral and—most probably—paranoid. How much of an influence did this have on his son? We will never know to what extent the father's psychological aberrations impacted on the son's psyche and value system. Nevertheless, Herod Antipas grew up in an environment where any possible threat to his family's political power (and wealth and prestige) would be met with a swift and lethal response.

The public ministry of Jesus did not begin until well into Herod Antipas' reign, and there is no real evidence that Herod was resentful of Jesus—or felt threatened by Him. Little mention is made in Scripture of Herod Antipas' personality or understanding of Jewish tradition and history—especially as it pertains to the much-awaited arrival of God's Messiah. Perhaps he can best be described as aware of Jesus' growing popularity, and curious about the rumored miracles attributed to Him, but any thoughts he may have had beyond mere curiosity are open to speculation.

When Herod divorced his first wife Phasaelis, the daughter of King Aretas IV of Nabatea, to marry his second wife Herodias, he was openly criticized by Jesus' cousin, John the Baptist, for violating Jewish law and entering into an incestuous relationship. Herodias was Herod Antipas' niece and sister-in-law (the wife of his half-brother Herod II). Fearing that the influential Baptist's words might fan the flames of rebellion, Herod had John imprisoned and later executed by beheading him. So this confrontation between the two, while not centered specifically on the ministry of Jesus, could infer a sense of "bad blood" between the two families—assuming, of course, that Herod Antipas were aware that John and Jesus were cousins. At the very least, Herod did know that there was a connection between the two:

> *When Herod, the ruler of Galilee, heard about all the things that were happening, he was very confused, because some people were saying that John the Baptist had come back to life. Others were saying that Elijah had appeared, and still others that one of the prophets of long ago had come back to life. Herod said, 'I had John's head cut off, but who is this man I hear these things about?' And he kept trying to see Jesus. (Luke 9:7-9)*

Eventually, after Jesus was arrested and appeared before Pontius Pilate, the Roman procurator of Judea, Pilate, in turn, sent Jesus to Herod, since Jesus was a Galilean, from the province ruled by Herod. This encounter was the only face-to-face meeting between the two, and Herod's treatment of Jesus was less than cordial:

> Herod was very pleased when he saw Jesus, because he had heard about him and had been wanting to see him for a long time. He was hoping to see Jesus perform some miracle. So Herod asked Jesus many questions, but Jesus made no answer. The chief priests and the teachers of the Law stepped forward and made strong accusations against Jesus. Herod and his soldiers made fun of Jesus and treated him with contempt... (Luke 23:8-11)

How could Herod Antipas and Manaen—the closest of friends and confidants—be raised side-by-side in an environment where one of them—Herod—killed Jesus' cousin and later mocked Jesus, and the other—Manaen—became a fervent supporter of Jesus and preached of His Resurrection and Ascension to others? Rev. Adam Orr of the Westside Church of Christ in Midland, Texas raised the question: "Who taught

Manaen about Jesus? Who shared the gospel with him? We don't know, the Word of God does not tell us. However, we do know that someone shared Jesus and salvation in Him with this future teacher."

One theory about Manaen's embrace of the Gospel is that he was influenced by another person connected loosely with Herod:

> *Some time later Jesus traveled through towns and villages, preaching the Good News about the Kingdom of God. The twelve disciples went with him, and so did some women who had been healed of evil spirits and diseases: Mary (who was called Magdalene), from whom seven demons had been driven out, Joanna, whose husband Chuza was an officer in Herod's court, and Susanna, and many other women who used their own resources to help Jesus and His disciples. (Luke 8:1-3)*

If Jesus had indeed cured Joanna of "evil spirits" (most likely either an emotional or psychological condition) or a physiological disease, there is an excellent chance that Manaen may have become aware of this either through Chuza or Joanna. And if this cure was viewed as miraculous, that would have made it all the more impressive and faith-inspiring. Of course, this connection is simply speculative, but it would suggest the presence in Herod's court of a positive and respectful view of Jesus —and perhaps even Herod's curiosity about Him. But whether or not there was a connection with the cure of Joanna that impacted Manaen, it *is* clear that Manaen not only became a disciple of Jesus, but a leader as well—and both a prophet and teacher of great importance to the growing Christian community at Antioch. As religious researcher and author Theresa Doyle-Nelson suggested in the *National Catholic Reporter*, "It is likely that he [Manaen] arrived in Antioch following the persecution of St. Stephen...Some consider that Manaen was probably one who introduced the teachings of Jesus to the people of Antioch, including the Gentiles there, who embraced Christianity in large numbers."

CHAPTER 6: QUESTIONS FOR REVIEW

1. Beside Simon Niger, what other *New Testament* figures are referred to by their physical characteristics, interests or occupations?
2. What does the prominence of Simeon in the Antioch Christian community say about the selection of leaders in the early Church?
3. Why do some religious historians see a connection between Simeon Niger and Simon the Cyrene?
4. What is the connection between the stoning of St. Stephen and the founding of the Church at Antioch?
5. Is there a connection between Lucius of Cyrene and St. Luke the Evangelist?
6. What kind of ruler was Herod the Great, the father of Herod Antipas?
7. What was the nature of the relationship between Manaen and Herod Antipas?
8. How would one characterize the feelings that Herod Antipas had toward John the Baptist and Jesus?

Chapter Seven
AGABUS

*"About that time, some prophets went from Jerusalem to Antioch.
One of them, named Agabus, stood up and...predicted..."*

It seems that many of the lesser known prophets of the *New Testament* were in some way, shape or form associated with Antioch, and Agabus is no exception. This should come as no real surprise, insofar as Antioch was one of the most important cities in the Roman Empire in the early days of the Church, eclipsed only, perhaps, by Rome and Alexandria. Agabus appears twice in the *Acts of the Apostles*, and in each case, under the inspiration of the Holy Spirit, he makes a dire prediction.

THE TROUBLING PREDICTIONS

The first prediction of Agabus inspired immediate and compassionate action on the part of the Christian community in Antioch:

> *About that time some prophets went from Jerusalem to Antioch. One of them, named Agabus, stood up and by the power of the Spirit predicted that a severe famine was about to come over all the earth. (It came when Claudius was emperor.) The disciples decided that each of them would send as much as he could to help their fellow believers who lived in Judea. They did this, then, and sent the money to the church elders by Barnabas and Saul. (Acts 11:27-30)*

It is important to note several things in this introduction to Agabus. First, he is referred to as a prophet in Scripture. Second, he is instantly recognized as one who is in receipt of the gift of the Holy Spirit, Who has conveyed a message to him about an upcoming event of great significance. Third, the validity of his prediction is accepted without question or discussion. And fourth, the consequences of this catastrophe on others demands a swift and generous response from those assembled to hear the prediction and they rise to the occasion willingly.

It is the second prediction of Agabus that has led to an ongoing debate within the Christian community over the last five centuries about the nature and tenure of prophecy itself, although this debate would have been unheard of at the time of the original prophecy:

> *We had been there* [in Caesarea] *for several days when a prophet named Agabus arrived from Judea. He came to us, took Paul's belt, tied up his own feet and hands with it, and said, 'This is what the Holy Spirit says: The owner of this belt will be tied up in this way by the Jews in Jerusalem, and they will hand him over to the Gentiles.' (Acts 21:10-11)*

When Agabus voiced this prediction, as with his first prediction about the upcoming famine, his words were taken at face value and thought to be truly inspired by the Holy Spirit and completely accurate. Those who heard the prediction immediately began to plead with Paul not to go to Jerusalem, but Paul disregarded their pleas, not because he questioned the validity of Agabus' prophecy, but rather because he was prepared to suffer—or even to die—for the sake of the Lord.

CESSATIONISM VS. CONTINUATIONISM

It was during the Protestant Reformation that this second prediction of Agabus began to serve as a lightning rod for discussion about the nature and duration of prophecy. Essentially, some theologians and Christian denominations began to fall into two different camps—*cessationism* and *continuationism*.

Cessationism is the belief that spiritual gifts such as speaking in tongues, prophecy and miraculous healing ceased with the Apostolic Age. This view is often attributed to such reformers as John Calvin, who believed that the Catholic Church's insistence that miracles and other dramatic spiritual occurrences such as the gift of tongues known as *glossolalia*) were designed to suggest a superiority of Catholicism over the emerging Protestant denominations. As a result, such sects as the Reformed and Presbyterian churches appeared to embrace cessationism in their theology.

Continuationism developed as a reaction to the cessationism of the Reformation. According to controversial evangelical pastor Mark Driscoll, "Continuationists believe that the sign gifts of the Spirit continue and have not ceased as the Spirit still works through gifts such as prophecy, knowledge, tongues, and healings in various ways. Sometimes continuationism is also referred to as being charismatic or Pentecostal." Those who embrace the continuational viewpoint, such as Dr. Wayne Grudem of Phoenix Seminary, believe in two types of *New Testament* prophecy. According to Nathan Busenitz of The

Master's Seminary, they [continuationists] believe, "There is *apostolic prophecy* which was infallible, authoritative, and foundational; it alone was equivalent to *Old Testament* prophecy, and it ceased after the time of the apostles...and there is a second type of *New Testament* prophecy—what we might call *congregational prophecy*. This form of prophecy is fallible, non-authoritative, and has continued throughout the church age. It is not equivalent to *Old Testament* prophecy."

What does this have to do with the second prediction of Agabus? Well, it all boils down to the way his second prediction is interpreted. Should one focus more on its exact wording or on the concept (spirit) behind the semantics? Agabus' statement that "the owner of this belt [Paul] will be tied up...and they [the Jews in Jerusalem] will hand him over to the Gentiles" did not happen literally as Agabus expressed it, so cessationists feel empowered to use this as proof that authentic prophecy did not extend beyond the time of the original twelve Apostles. Continuationists, however, will argue that while the details of Agabus' prediction may be literally inaccurate—or fallible (see above)—in terms of authentic prophecy, the overall sense of his prophecy is accurate. The debate between cessationists and continuationists will, most probably, be ongoing. After all, it's been a subject of debate for the past 500 years.

Religious writer JB Cachila, in his 2018 monograph "Who is Agabus in the book of *Acts* and what can we learn from him?" expressed his belief that, "Agabus' short appearances give us proof of how the Holy Spirit works...We see that the Holy Spirit knows the future...[and]...reveals the future to prophets...We see that when the Holy Spirit's message is received, it causes believers to respond...We learn from Agabus [that] prophets continued to exist after John the Baptist (contrary to what others claim)...[and]...prophets are mere men who listen to the Spirit of God."

CHAPTER 7: QUESTIONS FOR REVIEW

1. What was the first prediction made by Agabus, and how did his listeners respond to it?
2. What was Agabus' second prediction?
3. When and why did a debate emerge between cessationism and continuationism?
4. What is the cessationist view of prophecy?
5. In what ways do continuationists differ in their view of prophecy?

Chapter Eight
JUDAS BARSABBAS AND SILAS

*"Judas and Silas, who were themselves prophets, spoke a long time
with them, giving them courage and strength"*

The prophets Judas Barsabbas and Silas are first mentioned in the *New Testament* as part of the solution to a critical question that had emerged in the early Church. As mentioned earlier—and will be mentioned later as well—the subject of whether or not Gentile converts to Christianity would be required to conform to the dictates of Mosaic Law was an incredibly polarizing issue within the early Christian community. In the city of Antioch, a large number of Gentiles embraced faith in Jesus through the efforts of prophets and teachers such as Simeon Niger, Lucius of Cyrene, Manaen, Barnabas and Paul, and they were assured by Barnabas and Paul that conformity to Mosaic Laws, such as the requirement that the men be circumcised, would be unnecessary. Faith in Jesus would be sufficient for full and complete membership in the infant Church. But when other disciples (whose identities are unknown) arrived in Antioch with an opposite message, it set the stage for a confrontation and, hopefully, a timely resolution of the issue.

At a council of apostles and elders in Jerusalem, this controversy was discussed fully, and both Apostles Peter and James supported the viewpoint of Barnabas and Paul that Gentile conformity to Mosaic Law was unnecessary. The decision was then made to circulate this decision among the Gentile Christian communities that had emerged, and to do so both verbally and in writing.

JUDAS BARSABBAS

And this is where Judas Barsabbas and Silas first take center stage.

Then the apostles and the elders, together with the whole church, decided to choose some men from the group and send them to Antioch with Paul and Barnabas, They chose two men who were highly respected by the believers, Judas, called Barsabbas, and Silas, and they sent the following letter by them:

'We, the apostles and the elders, your brothers, send greetings to all of our brothers of Gentile birth, who live in Antioch, Syria and Cilicia. We have heard that some men who went from our group have troubled and upset you by what they said; they had not, however, received any instruction from us. And so we have met together and have all agreed to choose some members and send them to you. They will go with our dear friends Barnabas and Paul, who have risked their lives in the service of Our Lord Jesus Christ. We send you, then, Judas and Silas, who will tell you in person the same things we are writing. The Holy Spirit and we have agreed not to put any other burdens on you besides these necessary rules: eat no food that has been offered to idols; eat no blood; eat no animal that has been strangled; and keep yourselves from sexual immorality. You will do well if you take care not to do these things. With our best wishes.'

The messengers were sent off and went to Antioch, where they gathered the whole group of believers and gave them the letter. When the people read it, they were filled with joy by the message of encouragement. Judas and Silas, who were themselves prophets, spoke a long time with them, giving them courage and strength. After spending some time there, they were sent off in peace by the believers and went back to those who had sent them. (Acts 15:22-34)

The above citation is the only mention made of Judas Barsabbas in the *New Testament*, and it doesn't say a great deal about the man at face value. But it *is* possible to make several appropriate inferences about him that may add to our appreciation of him and his efforts. For example, the fact that Judas is described as "highly respected" by the apostles and elders in Jerusalem says a great deal about Judas' character. Clearly he had impressed the members of his own community with his service, his commitment and the depth of his faith. Second, Judas was sent to an emerging Christian community that was already troubled and confused by contradictory messages about their responsibilities and membership requirements in the church in Antioch. So Judas (along with Silas) were thought to possess the "diplomatic" skills and sensitivity to put this turbulence to rest and clarify the misunderstanding. Even though Judas was given a written letter of explanation and resolution to present to the Gentile Christians at Antioch, the apostles and elders were confident enough in Judas and Silas as representatives of the larger church to give them the freedom to offer any further clarifications and support that might be necessary.

Christian author and editor Bradley Cobb also pointed out in his 2015 monograph "Who was Judas Barsabbas?" that the selection of Judas to inform the Gentile Christians of Antioch that the Church was willing and eager to accept them into the faith as Gentiles rather than as "proselytized Jews" first also spoke of the character of Judas—that he was also eager to accept them as "brothers" exactly as they were.

And finally, the reference to both Judas and Silas as "prophets" clearly indicates that both men were thought to have received the gift of the Holy Spirit. Bradley Cobb further described Judas Barsabbas as "a Christian, baptized in order to have his sins forgiven, but he was also a preacher and an encourager...He is also a man upon whom the apostles laid their hands—he is called a 'prophet,' which means he has the miraculous ability to speak messages given to him by the Holy Spirit."

SILAS

While Silas and Judas Barsabbas are first introduced as emissaries to the Gentile Christian community in Antioch from the "mother" church in Jerusalem, this is only the beginning of the recorded ministry of Silas, while no further mention is made of Judas Barsabbas. When the time had come for Judas and Silas to depart Antioch, an argument between Barnabas and Paul caused them to split up. While Barnabas took John Mark with him to visit Cyprus, Paul invited Silas to accompany him on a journey to visit the other Christian communities that had emerged in some of the other towns in Syria and Cilicia.

Silas, like Paul, was a Roman citizen, but it's not known if his citizenship came through birth or purchase. His name is most likely related to the Roman name *Silvanus* or may be the Greek form of the Aramaic name *Seila*, which is a version of the

Hebrew *Saul*. It's unclear if Silas is his original name or an equivalent name from one of the other languages.

The letter that Paul, Barnabas, Judas and Silas had brought with them to Antioch was meant to be presented to all of the Christian communities in Syria and Cilicia as well, so Paul and Silas visited Derbe in Cilicia and Lystra in Pisidia to present the "good news" from Jerusalem and strengthen the local churches. It was in Lystra that they were joined by a young, highly-regarded Christian named Timothy, who accompanied them as they continued northward through Galatia and Phrygia. From Phrygia they continued west to the seaport of Troas in Mysia, where Paul had a vision that he and Silas were being called to preach in Macedonia. At Troas they boarded a ship for Samothrace and then on to Neapolis in Macedonia.

Macedonia was the setting for the first open hostility encountered by Silas. Paul had previously been stoned—and presumed dead—in Lystra on his first missionary trip with Barnabas, although, obviously, he survived that unfortunate episode. Upon their arrival at the inland city of Philippi, which also happened to be a Roman colony, *Acts* reported:

> *We were met by a slave girl who had an evil spirit that enabled her to predict the future. She earned a lot of money for her owners by telling fortunes. She followed Paul and us, shouting, "These men are servants of the Most High God! They announce to you how you can be saved!" She did this for many days, until Paul became so upset that he turned around and said to the spirit, "In the name of Jesus Christ I order you to come out of her!" The spirit went out of her that very moment. When her owners realized that*

their chance of making money was gone, they seized Paul and Silas and dragged them to the authorities in the public square. They brought them before the Roman officials and said, "These men are Jews, and they are causing trouble in our city. They are teaching customs that are against our law; we are Roman citizens, and we cannot accept these customs or practice them." And the crowd joined in the attack against Paul and Silas. (Acts 16:16-22)

The charges brought against Silas and Paul were only the first act of a much longer drama—a drama replete with violence, prayer, an act of God, conversion and apology.

The officials tore the clothes off Paul and Silas and ordered them to be whipped. After a severe beating, they were thrown into jail, and the jailer was ordered to lock them up tight. Upon receiving this order, the jailer threw them into the inner cell and fastened their feet between heavy blocks of wood.

About midnight Paul and Silas were praying and singing hymns to God, and the other prisoners were listening to them. Suddenly there was a violent earthquake, which shook the prison to its foundations. At once all the doors opened, and the chains fell off all the prisoners. The jailer woke up, and when he saw the prison doors open, he thought that the prisoners had escaped; so he pulled out his sword and was about to kill himself. But Paul shouted..."Don't harm yourself! We are all here!" (Acts 16:22-28)

Bradley Cobb concluded that, "The effects of the earthquake prove that it was miraculous. No natural earthquake could unlock chains around the feet of prisoners and open all the doors. Such a violent earthquake, one would assume, would also cause some serious damage to the structure, causing parts of it to crash into at least some of the prisoners, causing serious injury or even death. But there were no such incidents. It was an earthquake orchestrated and directed by God Himself, with only the effects that He wanted it to have."

As a result, the jailer began to sing a different tune. The drama of the earthquake coupled with the fact that the prisoners made no effort to escape, as well as their words of concern for the jailer, indicated that they were indeed messengers of God. This led him to drop to his knees and ask:

Sirs, what must I do to be saved? (Acts 16:30)

Paul and Silas replied:

Believe in the Lord Jesus and you will be saved—you and your family. (Acts 16:31)

Overjoyed, the jailer dressed the wounds of Silas and Paul, had his entire family baptized, and fed the "prisoners." The next morning the jailer received word from the Roman authorities to release Silas and Paul, but Paul would have none of it. He complained:

We were not found guilty of any crime, yet they whipped us in public—and we are Roman citizens! Then they threw us in prison. And now they want to send us away secretly? Not at all!

The Roman officials themselves must come here and let us out. (Acts 16:37)

When the officials realized they had severely mistreated two Roman citizens, they cowered in fear. Approaching Paul and Silas, they apologized, released them and requested that they leave the city. After bidding farewell to their supporters and offering them encouragement, Paul and Silas journeyed southwest to Thessalonica.

In Thessalonica, Paul and Silas preached about how Jesus had to suffer as the Messiah, and many Jews and Gentiles embraced the faith. However, other Jews—jealous at the attention Paul and Silas were receiving—formed a mob and tried to cause trouble, claiming that Paul and Silas were breaking imperial laws by claiming that Jesus was an alternate king. After being taken into custody and fined, they were released, but their supporters in Thessalonica sent Paul and Silas to Berea, which was southwest of Thessalonica, where they preached again to great success but were met again by the same Jew-incited mob that troubled them in Thessalonica. Supporters of Paul traveled with him as far as Athens to the southeast, but Silas and Timothy remained in Berea until they were summoned by Paul to join him in Athens.

At this point the timeline and locations both break down a little. It is thought that Silas may have journeyed to Philippi at Paul's request, but if this happened and over how long a period of time it happened is unknown. At some point Silas moved to Corinth, where he preached the Gospel—again for an unspecified period of time. And that is the last recorded word of the missionary travels of Silas.

Apparently, Silas' contributions to prophetic and missionary pursuits also extended to the written word. He, along with Paul and Timothy, are listed as the authors in the *First* and *Second Letters to the Thessalonians,* whose salutations both begin with the words:

> *From Paul, Silas and Timothy—to the people of the church in Thessalonica, who belong to God the Father and the Lord Jesus Christ... (1 Thessalonians 1:1)*

And finally, Silas is also credited with assisting in the composition of the *First Letter from Peter,* which begins with the words:

> *From Peter, apostle of Jesus Christ—to God's chosen people who live as refugees scattered throughout the provinces of Pontus, Galatia, Cappadocia, Asia and Bithynia... (1 Peter 1:1)*

and ends with the words:

> *I write you this brief letter with the help of Silas, whom I regard as a faithful Christian brother... (1 Peter 5:12)*

CHAPTER 8: QUESTIONS FOR REVIEW

1. Why did the church council at Jerusalem choose to send Judas Barsabbas and Silas to Antioch to deliver a written message of explanation?
2. While little information is presented in Scripture about Judas Barsabbas, what conclusions can be made about the character and value system of the man?
3. What is the significance of the Roman citizenship of Silas?
4. Why did Silas accompany Paul on his missionary journey from Cilicia to Macedonia?
5. Where and how did Silas and Paul first encounter hostility to their preachings?
6. How did an earthquake play a role in the conversion of a non-believer?
7. What were Silas' literary contributions to furthering the message of the Gospel?

Chapter Nine
SAUL (PAUL) OF TARSUS

*"In the church at Antioch there were some
prophets and teachers:
Barnabas...and Saul. the Holy Spirit said...
'Set apart for me Barnabas and Saul,
to do the work to which I have called them.'"*

*J*t is always a danger to rank individual persons or events in terms of their relative worth, contributions or accomplishments in the course of human events. But despite the inherent problems with such designations, it is not improper to single out Saul of Tarsus—also known as Paul—for his herculean efforts in introducing the Good News of Jesus to the Gentile world surrounding him. Many theologians and historians have ascribed the rapid spread of Christianity throughout the Mediterranean world and beyond to the efforts of Saul through his journeying, proselytizing and writing. It is no wonder that Saul (whom I will hereafter refer to as Saul and Paul interchangeably) has been gifted with the title "Apostle to the Gentiles."

The question has arisen: Is Paul a prophet? Professors Jacob M. Myers and Edwin D. Freed of the Lutheran Theological Seminary of Gettysburg College addressed this issue in 2016 in *Interpretation: A Journal of Bible and Theology*, when they wrote, "St. Paul is most widely known as the first great missionary of the Christian church—the Apostle to the Gentiles. A man of such vast experience exhibits many other characteristics of tremendous significance that formed the basic ingredients of his personality. He was an evangelist, teacher, preacher, theologian, traveler, tentmaker, churchman, as well as missionary—all indicative of the extraordinary qualities of that strange man from Tarsus. But nowhere in the *New Testament* Scriptures is he called a prophet, though there are numerous references to prophets. Although he himself does not claim to be a prophet or the possessor of prophetic powers, he frequently quotes from the canonical prophets, especially Isaiah, to support his views. It is [our] contention…that 'prophet of God' is also present among the many components in the personality of the Apostle Paul."

Again, it bears repeating that the concept of "prophet" as found throughout the *Old Testament* can and does take on new meaning and purpose when applied to those referred to as prophets throughout the *New Testament*—and especially so after the arrival of Jesus. In Paul's case, of course, his call to perform a specific task in relation to God's people came to him from the risen Christ Himself, rather than through the Holy Spirit, but entitled him to be regarded as a "messenger of God," the root definition of "prophet."

Paul's story is not only that of a gifted orator, brilliant mind and tireless worker—but it is first and foremost the tale of one of the most dramatic faith conversions in the *New Testament*, culminating in a dramatic shift from persecutor of the early Christian community to its greatest missionary and apologist.

PAUL'S EARLY LIFE

Born with the name of Saul in the city of Tarsus in Cilicia (in modern-day Turkey) in approximately 5 CE, Paul was born to Jewish parents who were Pharisees from the tribe of Benjamin. According to Professor Nils Dahl of the Yale Divinity School in his 1977 text *Studies in Paul*, "He was named for the tribe's most illustrious member, Saul, King of Israel. As was the case with many Hellenistic Jews, the boy also had a Greco-Roman name, the Latin Paulus." Paul's family possessed Roman citizenship, a privilege that would also extend to their son.

Details about the early life of Paul are rather sketchy, but it is thought that in about 10 CE, Paul's family moved from Tarsus to Jerusalem. Paul learned the trade of tentmaking as a means of supporting himself, but sometime between 15-20 CE, Paul began to study the *Hebrew Scriptures* in Jerusalem under the famous rabbi and scholar Gamaliel. Gamaliel was also a Pharisee and a member of the Jewish Council, the Sanhedrin. He was known for his rather lenient interpretation of the Jewish legal code of the *Old Testament* as compared with the more "hard-nosed" view of his contemporary, Rabbi Shammai. Interestingly, given the great influence Gamaliel had on Paul and Paul's early and energetic persecution of the early Church, it was Gamaliel who cautioned against such persecution, when he tried to stay the execution of Peter and John for spreading the Good News. At a meeting of the Sanhedrin, John and Peter were standing trial after having been warned to cease preaching in the name of Jesus. When Peter responded...

> *We must obey God, not men. The God of our ancestors raised Jesus from death, after you had killed Him by nailing Him to a cross. God raised Him to His right side as Leader and Savior, to give the people of Israel the opportunity to repent and have their sins forgiven. We are witnesses to these things—we and the Holy Spirit, Who is God's gift to those who obey Him. (Acts 5:29-32)*

...the Jewish council became enraged by Peter's defiance and sought the death of the apostles. Into the fray entered Gamaliel who ordered the apostles to be removed from the room. Gamaliel then suggested that the Council be cautious in dealing with Jesus' followers, saying:

> *In this case, I tell you, do not take any action against these men. Leave them alone! If what they have planned and done is of human origin, it will disappear, but if it comes from God, you cannot possibly defeat them. You could find yourself fighting against God. (Acts 5:38-39)*

The Sanhedrin was persuaded by Gamaliel's words and acquiesced to his advice. They had the apostles scourged and ordered them never again to speak in the name of Jesus, but the apostles remained undeterred and continued to proclaim the Good News.

THE STONING OF STEPHEN

As the Gospel message of Jesus continued to spread with more and more Judeans embracing the Christian faith, one of the leaders of the early Church, a man named Stephen, rose to a position of great prominence, and spoke with such wisdom and eloquence that his opponents were unable to refute him. So, Stephen's adversaries bribed a number of men to perjure themselves against Stephen, saying:

> *We heard him speaking against Moses and against God!...This man...is always talking against our sacred Temple and the Law of Moses. We heard him say that this Jesus of Nazareth will tear*

> *down the Temple and change all the customs which have come down to us from Moses! (Acts 6:11-14)*

Stephen was hauled before the Sanhedrin to explain himself, and launched into a lengthy oration about the details of the Covenant made between God and Abraham. The totality of his speech encompassed virtually all of Chapter 7 of the *Acts of the Apostles*. He traced the details of God's Covenant with His Chosen People through Abraham, Isaac, Jacob, Joseph, Moses, Joshua, David and Solomon, and ended his oration with the following indictment:

> *How heathen your hearts, how deaf you are to God's message! You are just like your ancestors: you too have always resisted the Holy Spirit! Was there any prophet that your ancestors did not persecute? They killed God's messengers, who long ago announced the coming of His righteous Servant. And now you have betrayed and murdered Him. You are the ones who received God's law, that was handed down by angels—yet you have not obeyed it! (Acts 7:51-53)*

If this accusation were not inflammatory enough, Stephen punctuated his remarks by looking up to heaven and exclaiming:

> *Look...I see heaven opened and the Son of Man standing at the right side of God! (Acts 7:56)*

Apoplectic with rage, the members of the Sanhedrin dragged Stephen out of the city and stoned him to death—the first recorded case of martyrdom for the Christian faith. But how does this relate to Paul?

> *The witnesses left their cloaks in the care of a young man named Saul...And Saul approved of his murder. (Acts 7:58-8:1)*

The murder of Stephen and Paul's participation in it—even if he threw no stones himself—marks Paul's introduction in the *New Testament*. Nils Dahl continued, "The dominating factor... which supplied the young Paul with a sense of direction, was Jewish in origin: his zeal for the Law. His service to the Law exceeded, at least in his own estimation, that of his pious contemporaries...Paul's zeal... led him to take an active role in persecuting those who confessed their faith in the crucified Messiah, Jesus of Nazareth...As a Pharisee, Paul found that the followers of the Nazarene weakened observance of the Law and diminished Israel's hope of entering the age to come. For the disciple of Gamaliel as for the apostle of Jesus Christ, there was an irreconcilable tension between the Mosaic Law and the crucified Messiah as ways to salvation."

Paul's passive involvement in the martyrdom of Stephen was a precursor to a much more active and virulent attack on Christians.

> *Saul tried to destroy the church; going from house to house, he dragged out the believers, both men and women, and threw them into jail. (Acts 8:3)*

As the church in Jerusalem began to suffer cruel persecution at the hands of Paul and others, the members of the church (except the apostles) started to scatter throughout Judea and Samaria. But Philip, Peter and John followed them to buttress their faith and bring new converts into the community. Paul, however, was relentless in his desire to crush the infant church.

> *Saul kept up his violent threats of murder against the followers of the Lord. He went to the High Priest and asked for letters of introduction to the synagogues in Damascus, so that if he should find there any followers of the Way of the Lord, he would be able to arrest them, both men and women, and bring them back to Jerusalem. (Acts 9:1-2)*

Paul was going to make it clear to the followers of Jesus that leaving Jerusalem would not prevent them from escaping his retribution.

THE CONVERSION OF PAUL

Armed with his letters of introduction and accompanied by a traveling party of like-minded vigilantes, Paul set out for Damascus on horseback, only to discover that a completely transformational experience awaited him.

> *As Saul was coming near the city of Damascus, suddenly a light from the sky flashed around him. He fell to the ground and heard a voice saying to him, "Saul, Saul! Why do you persecute Me?" "Who are You, Lord?" he asked. "I am Jesus, Whom you perse-*

cute," the voice said. "But get up and go into the city, where you will be told what you must do." (Acts 9:3-6)

While Paul's traveling companions heard the voice of Jesus, they saw nothing out of the ordinary. When Paul stood up, he opened his eyes only to discover that he was blind. His companions led him into Damascus, where he remained without sight for the next three days. During this time, Paul ate and drank nothing.

Paul's blindness was temporary, and served more as a "wake-up call" than a punitive measure. It was the first step in a transformational encounter that completely altered Paul's understanding of Jesus' role in salvation history.

While Paul—blind, fasting and emotionally and spiritually overwhelmed—contemplated his encounter with Jesus on the road to Damascus, another follower of Jesus was experiencing a like encounter of his own.

> There was a believer in Damascus named Ananias. He had a vision in which the Lord said to him, "Ananias!" "Here I am, Lord," he answered. The Lord said to him, "Get ready and go to Straight Street and at the house of Judas, ask for a man from Tarsus named Saul. He is praying, and in a vision he has seen a man named Ananias come in and place his hands on him so that he may see again. (Acts 9:10-12)

Ananias, an obedient and faithful disciple of Jesus, was undoubtedly honored by the task entrusted to him by the Lord —but was also troubled and fearful at the same time, as Paul's reputation for persecuting the followers of Jesus had preceded him to Damascus. He responded:

> Lord, many people have told me about this man and the terrible things he has done to Your people in Jerusalem. And he has come to Damascus with authority from the chief priests to arrest all who worship You. (Acts 9:13-14)

Nevertheless, the Lord had other plans for Paul, Ananias' warning notwithstanding.

> The Lord said to him, "Go, because I have chosen him to serve Me, to make My name known to Gentiles and kings and to the people of Israel. And I myself will show him all that he must suffer for My sake." (Acts 9:15-16)

Ananias needed no further convincing. The Lord's instructions were more than enough.

> So Ananias went, entered the house where Saul was, and placed his hands on him. "Brother Saul," he said, "the Lord has sent me —Jesus Himself, Who appeared to you on the road as you were coming here. He sent me so that you might see again and be filled with the Holy Spirit." At once, something like fish scales fell from Saul's eyes, and he was able to see again. He stood up and was baptized; and after he had eaten, his strength came back. (Acts 9:17-19)

The transmogrification of Paul was now complete—from utter rejection of Jesus to total acceptance, from extreme doubt to deep faith, from judge/jury/executioner to advocate and defender. But the metamorphosis of Paul—while authentic—was met with a great deal of suspicion by the members of the emerging Christian community. Was this some sort of trick—a "red herring" with an unknown and sinister hidden agenda? How could someone change his attitude and disposition so completely—virtually overnight? Is it any wonder that Paul's transformation was met with intense skepticism by the followers of Jesus who had either personally faced his acts of persecution or had heard of them from others?

Clearly, Paul needed to prove himself as a genuine believer, and he set out immediately and forthrightly to do so.

> *Saul stayed for a few days with the believers in Damascus. He went straight to the synagogues and began to preach that Jesus was the Son of God. All who heard him were amazed and asked, "Isn't he the one who in Jerusalem was killing those who worship that man Jesus? And didn't he come here for the very purpose of arresting those people and taking them back to the chief priests? (Acts 9:19-21)*

So Paul had a credibility issue that he needed to address, and he accomplished this in dramatic fashion, so much so that he found himself marked for death by the Jews who had previously been his most ardent supporters.

> *But Saul's preaching became even more powerful, and his proofs that Jesus was the Messiah were so convincing that the Jews who lived in Damascus could not answer him. After many days had*

> *gone by, the Jews met together and made plans to kill Saul, but he was told of their plan. Day and night they watched the city gates in order to kill him. But one night Saul's followers took him and let him down through an opening in the wall, lowering him in a basket. (Acts 9:22-25)*

Paul managed to establish himself as a follower of Jesus during his time in Damascus, and the genuineness of his conversion earned him a coterie of followers who successfully assisted him in leaving the city covertly and safely. But Paul's next step was to present himself to the Church leaders in Jerusalem, who were likewise suspicious of his possibly disingenuous motives.

> *Saul went to Jerusalem and tried to join the disciples. But they would not believe that he was a disciple, and they were all afraid of him. (Acts 9:26)*

Chapter 5 of this text introduced the prophet Barnabas, the bulk of whose prophetic ministry was spent with Paul on their missionary journeys together. While much of their ministry must be presented jointly, each of them also has a number of individual "adventures" and experiences unique to themselves. But it is at this moment that Barnabas plays a pivotal role in securing Paul's acceptance by the Church leaders in Jerusalem.

> *Then Barnabas came to his help and took him to the apostles. He explained to them how Saul had seen the Lord on the road and that the Lord had spoken to him. He also told them how boldly Saul had preached in the name of Jesus in Damascus. And so Saul stayed with them and went all over Jerusalem, preaching boldly*

> *in the name of the Lord. He also talked and disputed with the Greek-speaking Jews, but they tried to kill him. When the believers found out about this, they took Saul to Caesarea and sent him away to Tarsus. (Acts 9:26-30)*

For the second time, Paul convinced the Christian faithful of the legitimacy of his conversion. Not only did the boldness of his preaching in Jerusalem offer proof positive of his conviction, but the care the early Christian church took of Paul in removing him from Jerusalem when his life was threatened demonstrated that Paul had earned his complete acceptance into the fold.

Luke's *Acts* suggests that the Christian community entered into a period of relative peace and growth. Peter traveled a great deal, visiting the cities of Lydda and Joppa and, in response to an angelic visitation, journeyed to the home of the Roman captain Cornelius in Caesarea to preach the Good News at his invitation. When the Gentiles to whom Peter spoke were gifted with the Holy Spirit and began to speak in tongues, Peter and the six Christians from Joppa who accompanied him were amazed that Gentiles had received the gift of the Spirit—and Peter then proceeded to baptize all of them. This experience in Caesarea became a pivotal moment in the development and growth of the early Church. It was at this moment that Peter came to realize that the Good News and the Kingdom of God were not destined exclusively for Christians of Jewish ancestry, but for Gentiles as well. Upon his return to Jerusalem, when Peter recounted this episode, those who were initially horrified that Peter had defiled himself by consorting with Gentiles reversed themselves completely:

> *When they heard this, they stopped their criticism and praised God, saying, "Then God has given to the Gentiles also the opportunity to repent and live!" (Acts 11:18)*

The realization that the Good News was meant to be preached to the Gentile world as well as to the community of Israel, and that the gift of the Holy Spirit was being given to Gentiles as well as Jews, set the stage for the future missionary journeys of Paul and his singular designation as the great "Apostle to the Gentiles."

While Peter was introducing the Good News to the Gentiles at Caesarea, a city on the coast of the Mediterranean Sea northwest of Jerusalem in Samaria, other Christians who had settled far to the north in Antioch, Syria were similarly proclaiming the Good News to the Gentile community there—with startling results:

> *Other believers, men from Cyprus and Cyrene, went to Antioch and proclaimed the message to Gentiles also, telling them the Good News about the Lord Jesus. The Lord's power was with them, and a great number of people believed and turned to the Lord. (Acts 11:20-21)*

Antioch developed into a major center of Christianity as the years passed, and it was at Antioch that the title "Christians" was first used to describe the followers of Jesus. When the church in Jerusalem first heard the news of the growth of the Christian community in Antioch, the church leadership dispatched Barnabas to Antioch—and his efforts assisted the church in Antioch to grow further. Barnabas traveled to Tarsus to bring Paul back to Antioch, and the two of them continued to teach and preach for the following year. When another prophet named Agabus (see Chapter 7) predicted a severe upcoming famine, the Christians of Antioch pooled their resources to send aid to the Christian community in Judea, and the funds were brought to the church elders in Jerusalem by Barnabas and Paul, who then returned to Antioch to continue their work.

PAUL'S FIRST MISSIONARY JOURNEY

Upon their return to Antioch, Paul and Barnabas were singled out by the Holy Spirit for a special assignment, which proved to be Paul's first journey of proselytization to the Gentile world.

> *In the church at Antioch there were some prophets and teachers: Barnabas, Simeon (called the Black), Lucius (from Cyrene), Manaen (who had been brought up with Governor Herod) and Saul. While they were serving the Lord and fasting, the Holy Spirit said to them, "Set apart for me Barnabas and Saul, to do the work to which I have called them." They fasted and prayed, placed their hands on them, and sent them off. (Acts 13:1-3)*

Chapter 5 introduced the prophet Barnabas, who accompanied Paul on this first journey, but while Chapter 5 focused on the unique contributions of Barnabas, this chapter will place its primary emphasis on the singular efforts of Paul as this missionary journey unfolded. Paul and Barnabas set sail for the island of Cyprus, where they landed at the port of Salamis and preached in that city's synagogues. They were assisted in their efforts by the disciple John Mark as well.

Paul, Barnabas and John Mark traveled across Cyprus to the west coast port of Paphos, where they encountered a false prophet named Bar-Jesus, who was a friend of Sergius Paulus, the governor of Cyprus. *Acts* describes Bar-Jesus as a "magician" who did not want Sergius Paulus to hear the words of Paul and accept the faith.

> *Then Saul—also known as Paul—was filled with the Holy Spirit; he looked straight at the magician and said, "You son of the Devil! You are the enemy of everything that is good. You are full of all kinds of evil tricks, and you always keep trying to turn the Lord's truths into lies! The Lord's hand will come down on you now; you will be blind and will not see the light of day for a time." At once Elymas [the Greek name of Bar-Jesus] felt a dark mist cover his eyes, and he walked around trying to find someone to lead him by the hand. When the governor saw what had happened, he believed, for he was greatly amazed at the teaching about the Lord. (Acts 9-12)*

From Paphos in Cyprus, Paul and his two companions sailed to Perga, a city in Pamphylia to the northwest. Here John Mark left Paul and Barnabas to return to Jerusalem while Paul and Barnabas continued their journey to the city of Antioch in Pisidia (not to be confused with Antioch, Syria), where Paul addressed both Israelites and Gentiles alike. A number of converts were made in Antioch, but others objected to their preachings and banished them. Paul and Barnabas then proceeded northeast to Iconium, where the situation repeated itself. Paul and Barnabas spoke boldly to both Jews and Gentiles, many of whom accepted the faith. They also performed miracles, but others who refused to accept their preachings attempted to stone them. Paul and Barnabas fled to the city of Lystra in Lycaonia (in Asia Minor—which is modern day south central Turkey), where they preached the Good News.

In Lystra, Paul healed a crippled man who had been lame from birth, and the Lycaonian crowd who witnessed this healing began to view Paul and Barnabas as gods.

> *They started shouting in their own Lycaonian language, "The gods have become like men and have come down to us!" They gave Barnabas the name Zeus, and Paul the name Hermes, because he was the chief speaker. The priest of the god Zeus, whose temple stood just outside the town, brought bulls and flowers to the gate, for he and the crowd wanted to offer sacrifice to the apostles. (Acts 14:11-13)*

Paul and Barnabas were horrified by this attempt to deify them and pleaded with the people of Lystra to stop their adulation.

> *They tore their clothes and ran into the middle of the crowd, shouting, "Why are you doing this? We ourselves are only human beings like you! We are here to announce the Good News, to turn you away from these worthless things to the living God, Who*

> *made heaven, earth, sea, and all that is in them....He has always given evidence of His existence by the good things He does: He gives you rain from heaven and crops at the right times; He gives you food and fills your hearts with happiness." Even with these words the apostles could hardly keep the crowd from offering a sacrifice to them. (Acts 14:14-18)*

Despite the high regard in which Paul was held by the people of Lystra, Jewish dissidents arrived from Antioch, Pisidia and Iconium and turned the crowd against Paul. Paul was stoned and dragged out of the town by the crowd that thought he was dead, but Paul arose and returned to the town. But the next day Paul and Barnabas moved on to the town of Derbe, which was southeast of Lystra, where they preached the Good News and won many disciples.

Displaying great courage and faith, Paul and Barnabas chose to return to the cities they had previously visited—including Lystra, Iconium and Antioch, all of which had banished them—to strengthen and encourage the infant Christian communities they had helped to establish. They re-traced their steps all the way back to Antioch, Syria, the city from which their first missionary journey embarked, where they related their successes with the Gentile community. They remained in Antioch for an unspecified period of time, when a new controversy demanded their return to Jerusalem.

When men from the Christian community in Judea arrived in Antioch, they taught that salvation could not be attained unless the Law of Moses was observed through circumcision. When Paul and Barnabas strongly disagreed with this position, the stage was set for a return to Jerusalem to settle the matter with the apostles and elders. Even in Jerusalem there were some who believed in the necessity of circumcision.

> *Some of the believers who belonged to the party of the Pharisees stood up and said, "The Gentiles must be circumcised and told to obey the Law of Moses." (Acts 15:5)*

In the debate that ensued, Peter reminded the assemblage that God had called him to preach to the Gentiles and that the Gentiles had been freely gifted with the Holy Spirit because of their faith, with no other requirements such as circumcision required of them. Paul and Barnabas followed Peter with an accounting of their own miracles among the Gentiles and the inroads they had made in spreading the Good News among them. James, the leader of the church in Jerusalem, then expressed his opinion that further Mosaic demands should not be placed on the Gentiles, but rather that:

> *We should write a letter telling them not to eat any food that is ritually unclean because it has been offered to idols; to keep themselves from sexual immorality; and not to eat any animal that has been strangled, or any blood. (Acts 15:20)*

Paul and Barnabas, accompanied by two other prophets, Judas Barsabbas and Silas, were commissioned to bring this letter to the Christian community at Antioch, where the letter was met with great acceptance and joy. After spending some time in Antioch, Paul prepared for yet another foray into the Gentile world.

PAUL'S SECOND MISSIONARY JOURNEY

When Paul suggested to Barnabas that the two of them should revisit each of the towns in which they had previously preached the Good News, an argument erupted between the two that resulted in them severing their "partnership." Barnabas wanted to include young John Mark on their journey, but Paul was opposed to this because John Mark had left them abruptly in Perga on their last journey to return to Jerusalem. Barnabas wanted to give him another chance to redeem himself. The result of this disagreement was that Barnabas and John Mark sailed westward to Cyprus while Paul chose Silas as his companion and headed through Syria and Cilicia to the east.

After visiting and strengthening the fledgling Christian communities in Syria and Cilicia, Paul and Silas traveled west to Derbe and Lystra in Lycaonia. In Lystra, Paul met Timothy, a young Christian who was highly regarded by his neighbors and friends, and encouraged him to accompany them.

> *As they went through the towns, they delivered to the believers the rules decided upon by the apostles and elders in Jerusalem, and they told them to obey these rules. So the churches were made stronger in the faith and grew in numbers every day. (Acts 16:4-5)*

Dr. Frank W. Beare, professor emeritus of New Testament Studies at Trinity College in Toronto, related the next segment of their missionary trip in his 1962 text *St. Paul and His Letters*, when he wrote, "The three moved onward through the border regions of Galatia and Phrygia, looking for a new field of mission, always seeking the guidance of the Spirit of Jesus. At last they came to Troas, the most westerly port of the Asian coast, not far from the straits which we call the Dardanalles, and there they received the clear lead which they had been awaiting."

> *Paul had a vision in which he saw a Macedonian standing and begging him, "Come over to Macedonia and help us!" As soon as Paul had this vision, we got ready to leave for Macedonia, because we decided that God had called us to preach the Good News to the people there. (Acts 16:9-10)*

Dr. Beare summarized the remainder of Paul's journey by highlighting his evangelical successes and the church communities he founded. "The next few years were to witness a great movement of evangelization in the provinces of Macedonia, Achaea (Greece) and Asia (the western regions of Asia Minor). We hear of the founding of churches in Philippi, Thessalonica and Berea, all in Macedonia; of an unsuccessful attempt to win the leaders of thought in Athens, and of a long mission in Corinth which created a large and somewhat turbulent body of Christian believers in the capital city of Achaea; and then of a still longer mission centered in Ephesus, when 'all the people of Asia, both Jews and Greeks, heard the word of the Lord.' (*Acts 19:10*). The churches of the Lycus valley—Hierapolis, Laodicea and Colossae—were founded at this time by a young man trained by Paul, Epaphras of Colossae (*Col 1:7-8, 4:12-13*). Paul himself tells us that he carried the gospel message as far as Illyricum

(*Rom 15:19*), but *Acts* has nothing to say about this more distant expedition. This was the most fruitful period of Paul's life."

Paul's journey throughout the towns and cities of Macedonia, Achaea and Asia yielded a number of memorable and noteworthy encounters and events. In Philippi, Paul baptized a cloth merchant named Lydia and all the members of her household. He also encountered a slave girl possessed by an evil spirit that enabled her to predict the future. She used this power to earn a great deal of money for her owners, but Paul cast the evil spirit from her and brought her prognostications to an end. This set the stage for both pain and redemption.

> *When her owners realized that their chance of making money was gone, they seized Paul and Silas and dragged them to the authorities in the public square. They brought them before the Roman officials and said, "These men are Jews, and they are causing trouble in our city. They are teaching customs that are against our law; we are Roman citizens and we cannot accept these customs or practice them." And the crowd joined in the attack...Then the officials tore the clothes off Paul and Silas and ordered them to be whipped. After a severe beating, they were thrown into jail, and the jailer was ordered to lock them up tight....the jailer threw them into the inner cell and fastened their feet between heavy blocks of wood. (Acts 16:19-24)*

While the pain, violence and degradation were humiliating, it nevertheless set the stage for surprise, divine intervention and further conversion.

> About midnight Paul and Silas were praying and singing hymns to God, and the other prisoners were listening to them. Suddenly there was a violent earthquake, which shook the prison to its foundations. At once all the doors opened, and the chains fell off all the prisoners. The jailer woke up, and when he saw the prison doors open, he thought that the prisoners had escaped, so he pulled out his sword and was about to kill himself. But Paul shouted..."Don't harm yourself! We are all here!" The jailer...fell trembling at the feet of Paul and Silas. Then he led them out and asked, "Sirs, what must I do to be saved?" They answered, "Believe in the Lord Jesus and you will be saved—you and your family." Then they preached the word of the Lord to...all...in the house....The jailer...washed their wounds, and he and all his family were baptized at once. (Acts 16:25-33)

This episode—which started out quite badly before evolving into a moment of dramatic conversion—could have ended here, with Paul and Silas vacating the city. But it did not. Paul used this circumstance to "play the Roman citizen card," and not for the only time.

> The next morning the Roman authorities sent police officers with the order, "Let those men go."...but Paul said to the police officers, "We were not found guilty of any crime, yet they whipped us in public—and we are Roman citizens! Then they threw us in prison. And now they want to send us away secretly? Not at all! The Roman officials themselves must come here and let us out." The police officers reported these words to the Roman officials, and when they heard that Paul and Silas were Roman citizens, they were afraid. So they went and apologized to them, then they

> *led them out of the prison and asked them to leave the city." (Acts 16:35-40)*

Paul and Silas left Philippi and continued east to the city of Thessalonica, where Paul preached in the synagogue and converted many to follow Jesus. But other Jews formed a mob against Paul and Silas and attacked the house of Jason, which was hosting them. The mob accused them of sedition.

> *They are all breaking the laws of the Emperor, saying that there is another king, whose name is Jesus. (Acts 17:7)*

Jason and other members of his household were dragged before the town magistrates, who fined them and released them. After nightfall, Paul and Silas left Thessalonica for the town of Berea to the southwest, where Paul again spoke in the synagogue and converted many to the way of Jesus. But when the Jews who had incited the rioting in Thessalonica heard that Paul and Silas were preaching in Berea, they repeated their rabble-rousing ways and incited more chaos. Paul was escorted to Athens by some of the believers while Silas and Timothy remained in Berea. But Paul left instructions for them to join him in Athens at the earliest moment possible.

Upon his arrival in Athens, Paul was dismayed by the large number of idols in and around the city. As was his custom, he held discussions in the synagogue with some of the Athenian Jews—as well as with Gentiles, including some Epicurean and Stoic teachers. Paul was brought before the legislative council of Athens, the Areopagus, and asked to explain his "strange" teachings. So he addressed the Areopagus.

> I see that in every way you Athenians are very religious. For as I walked through your city and looked at the places where you worship, I found an altar on which is written, 'To an Unknown God.' That which you worship, then, even though you do not know it, is what I now proclaim to you. God, Who made the world and everything in it, is Lord of heaven and earth and does not live in man-made temples. Nor does He need anything that we can supply by working for Him, since it is He Himself Who gives life and breath and everything else to everyone. From one man He created all races of mankind and made them live throughout the whole earth. He Himself fixed beforehand the exact times and the limits of the places where they would live. He did this so that they would look for Him, and perhaps find Him as they felt around for Him. Yet God is actually not far from any one of us; as someone has said, "In Him we live and move and exist." It is as some of your poets have said, "We too are His children." (Acts 17:22-28)

Paul continued to address the council, explaining that God calls all people to reject their evil ways and will ultimately judge the whole world with justice through a man He has chosen—a man He raised from death. This revelation of Jesus' Resurrection elicited derision from some and acceptance from others, including Dioysius, a member of the Areopagus. Paul proceeded on to the city of Corinth.

In Corinth, Paul stayed at the home of Aquila and Priscilla, who moved to Corinth from Rome, after the Emperor Claudius had banished all the Jews from Rome. Skilled as a tentmaker, Paul worked with Aquila to earn his keep while also holding Sabbath discussions in the synagogue each week. Silas and Timothy joined Paul in Corinth, but Paul became frustrated by the Jews who opposed him and left the house of Aquila and Priscilla, moving instead into the house of a Gentile named Titius Justus. Eventually, Paul converted many to the ways of Jesus, buttressed by a vision of support he received one night.

> *The Lord said to him, "Do not be afraid, but keep on speaking and do not give up, for I am with you. No one will be able to harm you, for many in this city are My people." (Acts 18:9-10)*

As a result, Paul remained in Corinth for a year and a half, continuing to teach and preach the word of God. At the conclusion of his time there, Paul set out for Ephesus with Aquila and Priscilla, but did not remain in Ephesus at this time. He continued on to Jerusalem, where he greeted the members of the church, and then journeyed to Antioch.

PAUL'S THIRD MISSIONARY JOURNEY

Paul spent some time in Antioch, but then chose to revisit the Christian communities in Galatia and Phrygia in the hope of strengthening their faith. From there he continued west to Ephesus, a city he had visited briefly with Aquila and Priscilla during his second missionary journey. Upon his arrival, he discovered that the Good News message brought to the Ephesians was incomplete—they knew nothing of the Holy Spirit, and their understanding of baptism was confined to the baptism of John: to show repentance for their sins. They knew nothing of John's call to believe in the One Who would come after him—Jesus.

When the believers in Ephesus were baptized again in the name of Jesus, they were gifted with *glossolalia*, the ability to proclaim faith in God in other languages. Despite some who rejected his teachings about the Kingdom of God, Paul remained in Ephesus for over two years, giving both Jews and Gentiles throughout the province of Asia the opportunity to hear the word of God.

Paul's preachings in Ephesus were supported by a number of miracles attributed to him that enhanced his credibility with the people.

> *God was performing unusual miracles through Paul. Even handkerchiefs and aprons he had used were taken to the sick, and their diseases were driven away and the evil spirits would go out of them....The name of the Lord Jesus was given greater honor....Many of those who had practiced magic brought their books together and burned them in public. They added up the price of the books, and the total came to fifty thousand silver coins. In this powerful way the word of the Lord kept spreading and growing stronger. (Acts 19:11-20)*

Conversion is never easy nor automatic, and Paul's successes in Asia also led to controversy and, in the city of Ephesus, a virtual riot. Paul had arrived at the decision to travel to Macedonia and Achaia before returning to Jerusalem—and then to continue on to Rome. He sent his companions Timothy and Erastus ahead of him to Macedonia, while he remained a little longer in Ephesus. A silversmith named Demetrius began to foment anger at Paul and his teachings. As the leader of an enterprise that made silver idols of the goddess Artemis as well as models of her temple (which is considered one of the Seven Wonders of the Ancient World), he realized that Paul's preaching against man-made idols and the significant number of converts he had made would seriously damage Demetrius' business and the profits he was making. So Demetrius incited a large number of citizens by claiming that Paul's teachings would diminish the goddess Artemis. A mob grew in size and fury and the people began to chant "Great is Artemis of Ephesus!" While Paul wanted to address the crowd, his supporters would not allow it. Eventually a city clerk was able to calm the crowd and disperse its rabble rousers—and Paul was able to bid farewell to the believers and offer words of encouragement. With that, he left for Macedonia.

Paul passed through Macedonia, encouraging the communities of believers as he went. He stayed for three months in Achaia, but opted to return to Macedonia instead of journeying back to Syria, after hearing of a plot against him. Paul was accompanied by Sopater, Aristarchus, Secundus, Gaius, Tychicus, Trophimus and Timothy, all of whom joined him in Troas. It was in Troas that Paul was speaking with an assemblage of believers in the upper room of a residence when one of the attendees, a young man named Eutychus (who was sitting in a window well), became sleepier and sleepier—and fell out of a third story window—dying from the fall.

But Paul went down and threw himself on him and hugged him. "Don't worry," he said. "He is still alive!" Then he went back upstairs, broke bread, and ate. After talking with them for a long time, even until sunrise, Paul left. They took the young man home alive and were greatly comforted (Acts 20:10-12)

Paul departed Troas and traveled overland to the town of Assos, where he boarded a ship for the city of Mitylene on the northern Aegean island of Lesbos. From Lesbos he journeyed to the islands of Chios and Samo and debarked at Miletus on the west coast of the province of Asia (now Anatolia in Turkey). At Miletus, Paul sent a message to the elders of the church in Ephesus and, upon their arrival, used the opportunity to bid them farewell. He said:

And now, in obedience to the Holy Spirit I am going to Jerusalem, not knowing what will happen to me there. I only know that in every city the Holy Spirit has warned me that prison and troubles wait for me. But I reckon my own life to be worth nothing to me; I only want to complete my mission and finish the work that the Lord Jesus gave me to do, which is to declare the Good News about the grace of God...And now I know that none of you will ever see me again. (Acts 20:22-25)

It was Paul's intention to reach Jerusalem before the feast of Pentecost, but his journey proved to be a circuitous one. He and his companions boarded a ship that sailed past the islands of Cos and Rhodes, docking at the port of Patara. Here they boarded another ship bound for Phoenicia. They disembarked at the port city of Tyre in Syria, where they stayed with some believers for a week before continuing their ship voyage to Ptolemais and then Caesarea. In Caesarea, Paul stayed with Philip the evangelist and his daughters, but several days later Philip's household was visited by a prophet from Judea named Agabus (see Chapter 7).

> *He {Agabus} came to us, took Paul's belt, tied up his own feet and hands with it, and said, "This is what the Holy Spirit says: the owner of this belt will be tied up in this way by the Jews in Jerusalem, and they will hand him over to the Gentiles." (Acts 21:11)*

Paul's companions, hearing this prophecy, begged Paul to alter his plans, but Paul could not be dissuaded. He replied:

> *What are you doing, crying like this and breaking my heart? I am ready not only to be tied up in Jerusalem but even to die there for the sake of the Lord Jesus. (Acts 21:13)*

Upon Paul's arrival in Jerusalem, he was welcomed by James and the church elders, and he reported to them the successes he and his companions experienced among the Gentiles. But the elders were concerned that the Jews of Judea who had embraced the Way of Jesus had been led to believe that Paul had rejected the Law of Moses by telling the Jews in Gentile lands not to circumcise their sons or follow Jewish customs. So they asked Paul to perform a ritual of purification to demonstrate that he himself was living in accord with Mosaic Law. Paul acceded to this request, but just before the period of purification was about to come to an end, some Jews from Asia arrived and stirred up a mob against Paul.

THE PLOT AGAINST PAUL

As the riot grew larger and more boisterous, and Paul was dragged out of the Temple as the crowd began to beat him, Roman soldiers arrived on the scene to put down the disturbance. Confusion reigned, and the Roman commander Claudius Lysias heard a number of conflicting reports as to the cause of the riot. He then ordered Paul arrested and chained until he had a better grasp of the situation. As Paul was dragged to the headquarters of the Roman garrison, he was given permission by the commander to address the crowd. He introduced himself and gave a detailed explanation of himself, his respect for the Law of Moses, his initial opposition to those who chose to follow the Way of Jesus, his conversion on the road to Damascus, and the Lord's desire that he should spread the Good News in Gentile lands. Paul's speech only further inflamed the mob, and Claudius Lysias ordered Paul to be whipped.

When Paul informed the commander that he was a Roman citizen by birth, the commander feared the way he had treated Paul. Roman citizens could not be whipped or otherwise tortured, and they were entitled to a legal trial with a judge—and the right to appeal. The next day he had Paul brought before the High Priest Ananias and the Sanhedrin to ascertain why the Jews were so angry with Paul. When Paul began to speak, a quarrel erupted within the Sanhedrin, which consisted of Pharisees and Sadducees. Pharisees (such as Paul) believed in angels, spirits and resurrection from the dead, but the Sadducees did not. As the fight grew more violent, Paul was removed from the scene for his own protection. However, a number of Jews, forty in total, took a vow not to eat until they had killed Paul. Their plan was to execute the plot the following day.

When Claudius Lysias was informed of the plot, he sent a large number of soldiers, horsemen and spearmen to accompany Paul to Caesarea to present him to the territorial Governor Felix. He informed the governor in a letter that Paul was a Roman citizen who had done nothing to deserve imprisonment or death—that the accusations against him related to Jewish, not Roman, law. Felix decided to hold a hearing when Paul's accusers were able to arrive in Caesarea.

At Paul's hearing, Ananias, the Jewish elders and their lawyer Tertullus accused Paul:

> *We found this man to be a dangerous nuisance; he starts riots among the Jews all over the world and is a leader of the party of the Nazarenes. He also tried to defile the Temple, and we arrested him. (Acts 24:5-6)*

Paul defended himself and reminded Felix that it was Jews from Asia—and not Ananias and the Sanhedrin—who initiated the riot, and he challenged his accusers to specify what, if any, crimes he had committed, knowing that he was innocent of any wrongdoing. Felix closed the hearing and announced that he would render a decision upon the arrival of Claudius Lysias.

Paul was kept under guard but given some degree of freedom. Paul was thus kept in confinement for the next two years, at which time Felix was replaced as governor with Festus.

After two years of incarceration in Caesarea, Paul's status had not changed at all. When Festus visited Jerusalem, the chief priests appealed to him to send Paul to Jerusalem (where they had concocted another plot to kill him). While Festus wanted to ingratiate himself to the Jews, he told the accusers that they would have to come to Caesarea for another hearing. In Caesarea, history repeated itself: the chief priests levied the same charges, and Paul challenged them to offer proof of their claims, which they were unable to do. When Festus asked Paul if he would be willing to go to Jerusalem to be tried, Paul responded:

> *I am standing before the Emperor's own judgment court, where I should be tried. I have done no wrong to the Jews, as you yourself well know. If I have broken the law and done something for which I deserve the death penalty, I do not ask to escape it. But if there is no truth in the charges they bring against me, no one can hand me over to them. I appeal to the Emperor. (Acts 25:10-11)*

Festus consulted with his advisors and agreed to send Paul to the Emperor, but one more delay was destined to interfere. After Festus had been installed as governor and Paul was awaiting his journey to plead before the Emperor, King Agrippa II and his sister Bernice paid a visit of welcome to Festus. When Festus explained the charges brought against Paul and Paul's demand to speak to the Emperor, Agrippa wanted to hear Paul for himself. So Paul, in much the same way as he spoke of his background, conversion and ministry to Ananias, the Sanhedrin and Claudius Lysias, now addressed King Agrippa and Bernice. At the conclusion of his speech, Festus, Agrippa and Bernice all agreed that Paul had done nothing that merited either imprisonment or death. And Agrippa said:

> *This man could have been released if he had not appealed to the Emperor. (Acts 26:32)*

PAUL'S FINAL VOYAGE TO ROME

When Paul set sail for Rome to plead before the Emperor, the voyage was not an easy one. Under the supervision of a Roman officer named Julius, Paul and several other prisoners boarded a ship in the port city of Adramyttium and sailed past Cyprus to the port of Myra in Lycia. Here they changed ships and docked at Cnidus, where the high winds forced them to alter direction and dock at Lasea, on the south shore of the island of Crete. Paul foresaw that there would be great troubles ahead—damage to the cargo and ship, as well as loss of life—but no one heeded his warning. So from Lasea they continued under adverse weather conditions to the south shore of the small isle of Cauda.

The violent storm continued, and they were forced to throw cargo and ship equipment overboard. For days, the passengers and crew could not even see the sun or stars, and hopelessness prevailed. Paul tried to bolster their spirits:

> *Now I beg you, take courage! Not one of you will lose his life; only the ship will be lost. For last night an angel of the God to Whom I belong and Whom I worship came to me and said, "Don't be afraid, Paul! You must stand before the Emperor. And God in His goodness to you has spared the lives of all those who are sailing with you." So take courage, men! For I trust in God that it will be just as I was told. But we will be driven ashore on some island."*
> *(Acts 27:22-26)*

It was another fourteen days and nights before the crew saw an island in the distance and ran the ship aground once they spied a bay with a beachfront. They disembarked and soon discovered the island was Malta. The natives of Malta treated the ship's passengers and crew with a great deal of kindness. The island's chief, a man named Publius, was especially gracious and generous. When he told Paul that his father was ill with fever and dysentery, Paul went to visit him, prayed, laid his hands on him and cured him. After that, the other inhabitants of Malta who were ill also approached Paul and were healed, as well.

They spent three months on Malta and sailed to Syracuse on the island of Sicily on a ship from Alexandria that had spent the winter on the island. From Syracuse they reached the coast of Italy, sailing first to the southern port of Rhegium and then following the western coast northward to the town of Puteoli. One week later, after spending several days with believers in Puteoli, Paul reached Rome, where he was allowed to live by himself, with only a soldier guarding him.

After several days in Rome, Paul was permitted to call a meeting between him and the local Jewish leaders. Paul explained his ministry to them in detail and preached about Jesus, the Good News and the Kingdom of God and how he also preached the word of God to the Gentiles. Some accepted his teachings while others did not. This went on for two years, with Paul living by himself, welcoming all who came to visit him, and preaching the Good News. The date and manner of Paul's death is unknown, but there is universal agreement that he died a martyr's death. It is popularly thought that Paul was beheaded sometime between 62-64 CE under the authority of the Emperor Nero, more probably after the great fire in Rome in 64 CE for which Nero was responsible, although he placed the blame for it on the Christians of Rome.

THE PAULINE EPISTLES

It is unfair and incomplete to end a discussion of the life, ministry and death of Paul without also addressing his epistles. Of the 27 books that comprise the *New Testament*, 13 books are ascribed to Paul, whether written exclusively by himself or written by others who had access to his other compositions. The epistles of Paul constitute at least one-third of the *New Testament*, but when writings *about* Paul (such as in the *Acts of the Apostles*) are included, Pauline literature makes up almost half of the corpus of the *New Testament* and elevates Paul as the second most important figure in the history of Christendom. A brief summary of the topics he addressed in his epistles is necessary and proper.

It is universally recognized that Paul himself composed *1 Thessalonians, 1* and *2 Corinthians, Galatians, Philippians, Romans* and *Philemon*. While many argue that Paul personally wrote *all* of his epistles, some Biblical scholars maintain that *Ephesians, Colossians* and *2 Thessalonians* were actually composed by disciples of Paul who had access to some of his other writings—and used this access to extrapolate his thoughts. Still others view *1* and *2 Timothy* and *Titus* as compositions of other followers of Paul from a later date.

There is also no unanimity as to the exact order in which these epistles were composed—whether by Paul exclusively or by one or more of his associates. This is true especially at the advent of Paul's letters. Did he compose *Galatians* first, or did that epistle follow both *First* and *Second Thessalonians*? Either way, hopefully a brief summary of the epistles known to be composed by Paul may provide an insight into the message he brought so successfully to the Christian communities he established.

It is believed (by some) that the first epistle written by Paul was his *Letter to the Galatians*, a church he founded around 47-49 CE in what is now modern Turkey. Some believe this may have been written as early as 51 CE while others date it as late as 55-57 CE. In *Galatians*, Paul spoke of his call to spread the Good News to the Gentile community—a call he received from Jesus Himself, after having initially gone to great lengths to persecute the members of the Christian community. Paul emphasized in this letter that Gentile converts to Christianity—including those in the community of Galatia—were not required to "become Jews" by embracing Jewish customs or following Mosaic laws such as circumcision—that faith alone in Jesus was what was necessary for salvation.

Paul also placed great emphasis as well on the equality of all people:

> *So there is no difference between Jews and Gentiles, between slaves and free men, between men and women; you are all one in union with Christ Jesus. (Galatians 3:28)*

He also criticized the Galatian church for acceding to other self-proclaimed missionaries who encouraged them to adopt Mosaic practices in opposition to Paul's original preaching to them.

> *Listen! I, Paul, tell you that if you allow yourselves to be circumcised, it means that Christ is of no use to you at all...You are outside God's grace...For when we are in union with Christ Jesus, neither circumcision nor the lack of it makes any difference at all; what matters is faith that works through love. You were doing so well! Who made you stop obeying the truth? (Galatians 5:2-7)*

Clearly, Paul's disappointment in the willingness of these church members to wander from his original teachings had him very upset and discouraged.

Paul's second epistle (or perhaps his first) was the first of two composed for the church in Thessalonica, which was an important city as the capital of the Roman province of Macedonia. Some argue that Paul's *Second Letter to the Thessalonians* was actually written by one of Paul's disciples. Former *Christianity Today* editor Sam O'Neal pointed out that while Paul established a Christian community in Thessalonica, he spent very little time there, entrusting his companion Timothy to shepherd this new flock. Paul was unable to spend much time here—as a result of opposition from Jews who caused a great deal of turbulence and chaos. As such, Paul was forced to leave prematurely. When he received a communication from his companion Timothy, who remained in Thessalonica, he saw the need to write his *First Letter to the Thessalonians* to clear up some misconceptions.

After praising the Thessalonians for their acceptance of the faith despite persecution, Paul explained how much he wished to visit them again but was unable to do so—which is why he sent Timothy to them in his stead. Paul urged the community to live holy lives free of sexual immorality, to live quietly, mind their own business and earn their own living. Along with this, Paul also begged:

> *Pay proper respect to those who work among you, who guide and instruct you in the Christian life...Be at peace among yourselves... warn the idle, encourage the timid, help the weak, be patient with everyone...make it your aim to do good to one another and to all people. Be joyful always, pray at all times, be thankful in all circumstances. This is what God wants from you in your life in union with Christ Jesus. (1 Thessalonians 5:12-17)*

Paul also reminded the Thessalonians that those who have died believing in Jesus will rise from death at the coming of the

Lord, and those who are alive at the coming of Jesus will also be with the Lord—always.

It is unclear how soon after his first epistle Paul (or a different disciple of his) wrote his *Second Letter to the Thessalonians*. If Paul did indeed compose it himself, Paul acknowledged that this community was continuing to grow in faith and love despite suffering continuing persecution, and promised them that they would be rewarded while their tormentors would be punished.

He also attempted to clear up a misconception that many had that the "Day of the Lord" has already come. Paul assured them that this had not yet occurred—rather, the Lord's appearance would be preceded by the arrival of great wickedness and deceit. He foresaw:

> *The Wicked One will appear...The Wicked One will come with the power of Satan and perform all kinds of false miracles and wonders, and use every kind of wicked deceit...The result is that all who have not believed the truth, but have taken pleasure in sin, will be condemned. (2 Thessalonians 2:6-12)*

But Paul assured them that:

> *God chose you as the first to be saved by the Spirit's power to make you His holy people and by your faith in the truth. (2 Thessalonians 2:13)*

It *is* believed that Paul wrote as many as four letters to the church community in Corinth, a thriving cosmopolitan Greek city that served as the Roman capital of Achaia, but that only two have survived—the *First* and *Second Letters to the Corinthians*, both presumably written in 57 CE. Corinth was a trading center that included a population from diverse places practicing diverse religions. Gods and goddesses of Rome, Greece and Egypt were worshiped, with a special veneration offered to Aphrodite, the goddess of love, whose temple on a summit overlooking the harbor of Corinth featured over a thousand women who served as prostitutes. So it is no surprise that Corinth was also a hotbed (pardon the pun) of sexual immorality and hedonism. As a result, the primary problem faced by the emerging church in Corinth was not pressure to follow Jewish Mosaic customs as much as it was to steer the new church members away from the immoral practices of the metropolis.

Paul realized this. His first task was to end the internal quarreling and divisions that had erupted in the church, when he wrote:

> *Let me put it this way: each one of you says something different. One says, 'I follow Paul,' another 'I follow Apollos,' another, 'I follow Peter,' and another, 'I follow Christ.' Christ has been divided into groups! Was it Paul who died on the cross for you? Were you baptized as Paul's disciples?...Christ did not send me to baptize. He sent me to tell the Good News. (1 Corinthians 1:12-17)*

But his greater challenge was to keep the young church at Corinth on solid moral ground, rejecting the excesses that surrounded its members on all sides—especially excesses of a sexual nature. Paul did not mince his words when he wrote:

> *Now it is actually being said that there is sexual immorality among you so terrible that not even the heathen would be guilty of it. I am told that a man is sleeping with his stepmother!...You should be filled with sadness, and the man who has done such a thing should be expelled from your fellowship... I told you not to associate with immoral people. Now I did not mean pagans who are immoral or are greedy or who are thieves, or who worship idols. To avoid them you would have to get out of the world completely. What I meant was that you should not associate with a person who calls himself a brother but is immoral or greedy or worships idols or is a slanderer or a drunkard or a thief. Don't even sit down to eat with such a person. (1 Corinthians 5:1-11)*

Trying to convince the members of the Corinthian church that their lifestyle must be countercultural to the lifestyle of the other residents of Corinth, he emphasized:

> *Avoid immorality. Any other sin a man commits does not affect his body, but the man who is guilty of sexual immorality sins against his own body. Don't you know that your body is the temple of the Holy Spirit, Who lives in you and Who was given to you by God? You do not belong to yourselves but to God...so use your bodies for God's glory. (1 Corinthians 6:18-20)*

Paul also addressed a series of other questions and issues that had arisen from among the members of the church community. He urged them to settle disputes among themselves within their own community—and not to use "heathen" judges from outside. While he encouraged the unmarried and widows to remain unattached, he recognized that some would be better off marrying than "burning with passion." Paul also spoke against divorce and against eating any food that had been offered to idols. He thought it was a disgrace for a man to worship with his head covered and for a woman to worship without covering her head, customs that reflected the times.

The gifts of the Holy Spirit were discussed at length by Paul:

> *There are different kinds of spiritual gifts, but the same Spirit gives them. There are different ways of serving, but the same Lord is served. There are different abilities to perform service, but the same God gives ability to all for their particular service....The Spirit gives one person a message full of wisdom, while to another person the same Spirit gives a message full of knowledge. One and the same Spirit gives faith to one person, while to another person He gives the power to heal. The Spirit gives one person the power to work miracles; to another the gift of speaking God's message...To one person He gives the ability to speak in strange tongues, and to another He gives the ability to explain what is said. But it is one and the same Spirit Who does all this. (1 Corinthians 12:4-11)*

Paul placed great emphasis on how each person plays a different role in the church and has been gifted by the Spirit in different ways, but how all members should set their sights on the "more important gifts." And this was a prelude to one of the most well-known and beloved passages in the body of Pauline literature—the "more important gift" of love—and what it means:

> *Love is patient and kind; it is not jealous or conceited or proud; love is not ill-mannered or selfish or irritable; love does not keep a record of wrongs; love is not happy with evil, but is happy with the truth. Love never gives up; and its faith, hope and patience never fail. Love is eternal. (1 Corinthians 13:4-8)*

Before concluding this epistle, Paul also addressed the supreme importance of faith that Jesus did indeed rise from death—and that His resurrection has gained eternal life and salvation for all who believe in Him:

> *But the truth is that Christ has been raised from death, as the guarantee that those who sleep in death will also be raised...Someone will ask, How can the dead be raised to life? What kind of body will they have?'...What is made of flesh and blood cannot share in God's Kingdom, and what is mortal cannot possess immortality...When the last trumpet sounds, we shall all be changed in an instant, as quickly as the blinking of an eye. For when the trumpet sounds, the dead will be raised, never to die again...For what is mortal must be changed into what is immortal; what will die must be changed into what cannot die...Then the scripture will come true,: 'Death is destroyed; victory is complete! (1 Corinthians 15:20,35,50,52-54)*

Paul's *Second Letter to the Corinthians* was composed during Paul's third missionary journey, possibly while he was visiting Macedonia. In the first part of this epistle, Paul makes reference to his first letter to them, in which he chastised (some of) them for falling into a state of sexual immorality and rejecting his teaching about the unnecessity of adopting Mosaic laws to join the church as followers of Christ.

> *If that letter of mine made you sad, I am not sorry I wrote it. I could have been sad when I saw that it made you sad for a while, but now I am happy—not because I made you sad, but because your sadness made you change your ways. That sadness was used by God, and so we caused you no harm. For the sadness that is used by God brings a change of heart that leads to salvation—and there is no regret in that! (2 Corinthians 7:8-10)*

After assuring the community at Corinth of his love for them, Paul then asked them to contribute what they could to assist the needy brethren in Judea.

> *There is really no need for me to write you about the help being sent to God's people in Judea. I know that you are willing to help. And I have boasted of you to the people in Macedonia....Each one should give, then, as he has decided, not with regret or out of a sense of duty; for God loves the one who gives gladly. (2 Corinthians 9:1-2,7)*

In the final chapters of *2 Corinthians*, Paul defended his ministry as an apostle and cautioned the local church community not to be deceived by other false apostles who preached a message inconsistent with Paul's.

> *Those men are not true apostles—they are false apostles, who lie about their work and disguise themselves to look like real apostles of Christ. Well, no wonder! Even Satan can disguise himself to look like an angel of light! So it is no great thing if his servants can disguise themselves to look like servants of righteousness. In the end they will get exactly what their actions deserve. (2 Corinthians 11:13-15)*

The longest and most complete epistle of Paul is his *Letter to the Romans*, most probably written in 57-58 CE during his third missionary journey. It was Paul's hope to visit the growing Christian community in Rome and enlist their aid in helping him to continue on to establish a Christian community in Spain. Paul's letter to the Roman community was the only epistle he had written to a community he had not founded himself, and because of this, he may have felt obliged to present the full scope of his message of faith and salvation to them. Apparently, Paul already knew something of the Roman Christian community, possibly from his friends Aquila and Priscilla (among others) who had been expelled from Rome by a 49 CE edict from the Emperor Claudius.

It is ironic that so little is known about the emergence of the Christian community in Rome, nor is it known if this community was composed primarily of Jewish or Gentile Christians, insofar as the city was destined to become the center of Christianity for the next two millennia. Regardless of the composition of this community, Paul reveals his primary and central theme in writing at the very beginning of his letter:

> *The gospel reveals how God puts people right with Himself: it is through faith from beginning to end. As the scripture says, 'The person who is put right with God through faith shall live.' (Romans 1:17)*

Paul speaks about how God's divine nature is clearly visible in all that God has created, yet people fail to see this and choose to worship man made idols instead of God. The result of this is a wide array of shameful and sinful behaviors:

> *They do the things that they should not do. They are filled with all kinds of wickedness, evil, greed and vice; they are full of jealousy, murder, fighting, deceit and malice. They gossip and speak evil of one another; they are hateful to God, insolent, proud and boastful...they disobey their parents, they have no conscience; they do not keep their promises, and they show no kindness or pity for others. (Romans 1:29-31)*

For Paul, one does not become "right with God" by following the law—even the Law of Moses—but through faith in Jesus:

> *God puts people right through their faith in Jesus Christ. God does this to all who believe in Christ, because there is no difference at all: everyone has sinned and is far away from God's saving presence. But by the free gift of God's grace all are put right with Him through Christ Jesus, Who sets them free. (Romans 3:22-24)*

While Paul—before his conversion on the road to Damascus—was an ardent proponent of the Mosaic law and its integral role in salvation history, he had completely reversed his position and come to realize that the primary error made by the Jews in rejecting the Gospel message of Jesus was their failure to realize that:

> *Christ has brought the Law to an end, so that everyone who believes is put right with God. (Romans 10:4)*

The United States Conference of Catholic Bishops offered this summary of the epistle: "Paul's *Letter to the Romans* is a powerful exposition of the doctrine of the supremacy of Christ and of faith in Christ as the source of salvation. It is an implicit plea to the Christians at Rome, and to all Christians, to hold fast to that faith. They are to resist any pressure put on them to accept a doctrine of salvation through works of the law. At the same time they are not to exaggerate Christian freedom as an abdication of responsibility for others or as a repudiation of God's law and will."

The three remaining epistles that are ascribed to Paul (rather than to unnamed disciples of his)—the *Letter to the Colossians*, *Letter to the Philippians* and *Letter to Philemon*—were all composed while Paul was incarcerated in Rome, circa 62 CE. His epistle to the people of Colossae, a small town in the Roman province of Asia in the valley of the Lycus River, reveals several unique side stories. First, while Paul was ultimately responsible for the founding of a number of Christian communities in Asia, that does not necessarily mean that Paul personally visited these communities. Apparently, Paul trained and dispatched several associates to spread the Good News throughout Asia, and one of these disciples, Epaphras, was assigned to spread the Gospel message to the residents of the Lycus River Valley. And it was Epaphras who reported to Paul that a new and confusing teaching had found its way into the Valley—by whom was unclear—which needed to be refuted.

As Dr. Frank Beare pointed out in his 1962 text *St. Paul and His Letters*, "It is very difficult for us to make out the exact nature of this teaching, since we know nothing whatever about it except what we can gather from the letter itself, and Paul is not setting out to expound it, but only to refute it...The new teaching appears to be based upon a doctrine of angels—powerful cosmic spirits who are to be worshiped. They are called 'the elemental spirits of the universe' and are given a variety of names which may correspond to gradations of rank, as 'thrones, dominions, principalities, authorities.' Together they constitute the pleroma, or fullness, of divinity, as if the ineffable divine essence were unfolded through them. These mysterious beings were probably conceived as astral spirits, having their abode in the stars and controlling the destinies of men. They bring men 'redemption'...In the matter of conduct, this transcendental doctrine required a severe asceticism coupled with ritual and legal requirements which went far beyond the simple Christian laws of love and purity. It imposed taboos on certain forms of food and drink, and required the observance of 'festival, new moon and sabbath'—probably those laid down in the Mosaic law....There are indications that it required its adherents to be circumcised."

The problems faced by Epaphras—and also by Paul—are reminiscent of the problems faced by the community in Galatia when other unknown disciples of Jesus entered the scene after

Paul had left and tried to impose the requirements of Mosaic Law on the new Gentile Christians in Galatia. It appears that a similar occurrence has happened in Colossae—not only with an attempt to impose Mosaic customs and rituals on the newly converted, but with the introduction of a new doctrine implying the divinity of other celestial spirits who are worthy of the same worship accorded to Jesus. That is why Paul felt it necessary to proclaim most emphatically the salvific power and authority of Jesus alone:

> *Christ is the visible likeness of the invisible God. He is the first-born Son, superior to all created things. For through Him God created everything in heaven and on earth, the seen and the unseen things, including spiritual powers, lords, rulers and authorities* [or 'thrones, dominions, principalities and authorities]. *God created the whole universe through Him and for Him. Christ existed before all things, and in union with Him all things have their proper place. He is the head of His body, the church; He is the source of the body's life. He is the first-born Son, Who was raised from death, in order that He alone might have the first place in all things. For it was by God's own decision that the Son has in Himself the full nature of God.* (Colossians 1:15-19)

These words of Paul are uncompromising in their proclamation that no other types of spirits or celestial beings are in any way equal to Jesus or worthy of the same level of reverence and respect as Jesus. Paul goes on to speak specifically about—and to reject completely—the rituals and customs the Colossians were asked to observe by these other so-called disciples:

> *See to it, then, that no one enslaves you by...the teachings handed down by men and from the ruling spirits of the universe, and not from Christ...He is supreme over every spiritual ruler and authority...So let no one make rules about what you may eat or drink or about holy days or the New Moon Festival or the Sabbath...Do not allow yourselves to be condemned by anyone...who insists on...the worship of angels. (Colossians 2:8-10,16-18)*

Unlike Paul's *Letter to the Colossians*, his *Letter to the Philippians* was not composed to address any crisis or misunderstanding that had developed in the church at Philippi. It was written at the same time as the *Letters to Colossians* and *Philemon* (circa 62 CE) while Paul was imprisoned in Rome, awaiting his appeal to the emperor. The church at Philippi was the first Christian community founded by Paul in Macedonia and, as such, it was special to him. It was a church he visited twice—on his second and third missionary journeys.

The *Letter to the Philippians* gave Paul an opportunity to express his gratitude to the community for their material support of his ministry as well as his joy in celebrating the profundity of their faith, generosity and service to the Gospel. He opens his letter with this prayer that captures these feelings:

> *I thank my God for you every time I think of you; and every time I pray for you all, I pray with joy because of the way in which you have helped me in the work of the gospel from the very first day until now. (Philippians 1:3-5)*

After explaining how he is able to maintain a joyful demeanor while in prison—because he can see how his imprisonment is enabling his fellow evangelists to speak with increasing boldness about the Lord—Paul encouraged the Philippians by reminding them that:

> *You have fellowship with the Spirit, and you have kindness and compassion for one another...Don't do anything from selfish ambition or from a cheap desire to boast, but be humble towards one another, always considering others better than yourselves. And look out for one another's interests, not just for your own. The attitude you should have is the one that Christ Jesus had. (Philippians 2:1-4)*

And Paul goes on to describe the humble demeanor of Jesus and the greatness of Jesus that flows from that humility—using words that have resounded over the last two millennia that can be recited today by a great many Christians:

> *He always had the nature of God, but He*
> *did not think that by force He should try to*
> *become equal with God.*
> *Instead of this, of His own free will He gave*
> *up all He had, and took the nature of a servant.*
> *He became like man and appeared in human*
> *likeness. He was humble and walked the path*
> *of obedience all the way to death —*
> *His death on a cross.*
> *For this reason God raised Him to the highest*
> *place above and gave Him the name that is*

> *greater than any other name. And so, in honor*
> *of the name of Jesus all beings in heaven,*
> *on earth, and in the world below will fall*
> *on their knees,*
> *And all will openly proclaim that Jesus Christ*
> *is Lord, to the glory of God the Father.*
> *(Philippians 2:6-11)*

The last epistle universally recognized to have been written by Paul—also composed while in a Roman prison, circa 62 CE—is his *Letter to Philemon*. This epistle addresses for the first time in Paul's writings the institution of slavery, which was as pervasive in society then as it is abhorrent to us now. It should be noted that Paul does not condemn the institution of slavery in this letter nor does he make an appeal for the emancipation of slaves. The reasons for this are probably twofold. First, the infant church was not in a position to exert pressure on the Roman Empire to reverse an institution that was already embedded in the very fiber of Roman society. And second, Paul believed firmly that the second coming of Christ would occur in the very near future—perhaps months, or even weeks, away—and the issue would be addressed at that time. For Paul, the issue of slavery was reduced to the status of one man—a slave named Onesimus.

Onesimus was a slave who belonged to Philemon, a prominent and wealthy Christian in Colossae. He ran away from the house of Philemon and traveled to Rome, where he met Paul and was converted by him to faith in Jesus. It is unclear if Onesimus, in his escape, had stolen from Philemon and was thus further indebted to him.

Paul's *Letter to Philemon* (which is also addressed to Philemon's sister Apphia and a comrade named Archippus) does not ask Philemon to release Onesimus from slavery, nor does it condemn the institution of slavery. After praising Philemon for his great faith and love, Paul asks for a favor:

> *I make a request to you on behalf of Onesimus...while in prison I have become his spiritual father...I am sending him back to you now, and with him goes my heart...Now he is not just a slave, but much more than a slave: he is a dear brother in Christ. How much he means to me! And how much more he will mean to you, both as a slave and as a brother in the Lord! (Philemon 1:10-15)*

Paul also wrote to Philemon that he would welcome Onesimus remaining with him in Rome to assist Paul with his work, but does not wish to impose on Philemon—although he is confident that the very generous Philemon will grant his request. Paul also offers to pay Philemon from his own pocket for any money that Onesimus may owe Philemon.

Paul ends his epistle with words that may very easily be construed as polite arm-twisting accompanied by a dose of flattery when he writes

> *So, my dear brother, please do me this favor for the Lord's sake...I am sure, as I write this, that you will do what I ask—in fact I know that you will do even more. (Philemon 1:20-21)*

CHAPTER 9: QUESTIONS FOR REVIEW

1. What biographical information is available about the early life of Paul?
2. What case can be made for calling Paul a prophet—and for not doing so?
3. Why did Paul spend so much time and energy in persecuting the followers of Jesus?
4. What were the circumstances that led to Paul's conversion?
5. How did Paul act after his encounter with Jesus and introduction to Ananias?
6. How was Paul able to gain acceptance from the Church leaders in Jerusalem?
7. What successes did Paul achieve during his first missionary journey? Did he experience any moments of discomfort, frustration or failure?
8. What caused Paul to choose Silas to accompany him on his second missionary journey?
9. What approach was used by Paul in introducing Jesus to the people of Athens?
10. How many epistles are thought to have been written by Paul—and which ones are thought to have been composed by others?
11. Why was Paul critical of the church community in Galatia?
12. What guidelines for daily living were provided by Paul in his *First Letter to the Thessalonians*?

13. How did Paul address the issue of the arrival of the "Day of the Lord" in *2 Thessalonians*?
14. What problems had erupted in Corinth that required a reprimand and advice from Paul in his *First Letter to the Corinthians*?
15. What did Paul say in this same epistle about the gifts of the Holy Spirit?
16. According to Paul in *1 Corinthians*, what are the qualities of love?
17. In the *Letter to the Romans*, how does Paul suggest a person becomes "right with God?"
18. What new doctrine was preached in Colossae that Paul needed to refute? How did he refute it?
19. What issue was Paul required to address in his *Letter to Philemon*—and what request did he make?

Chapter Ten

JOHN OF PATMOS

*"Christ made these things known to His servant John
by sending His angel to him,
and John has told all that he has seen."*

Like so many other Biblical figures, John of Patmos is viewed in many different ways by scholars and theologians who are attempting to positively identify not only the man himself—but his writings as well.

Some scholars maintain that "John of Patmos" was none other than "John the Evangelist," also known as "John the Apostle" or "John the Divine"—a man selected by Jesus, along with John's brother James, to be included in the inner circle of Jesus' Twelve Apostles. If this is true, then Scripture does provide us with certain specific information about John. Others maintain, of course, that John of Patmos is a very different person who did not know Jesus personally as a member of His closest disciples.

ARE JOHN OF PATMOS AND JOHN THE EVANGELIST THE SAME PERSON?

If John of Patmos *was* John the Evangelist and Apostle, then some biographical information about him is available. John is first introduced when…

> *He [Jesus] went on and saw two other brothers, James and John, the sons of Zebedee. They were in their boat with their father Zabedee, getting their nets ready. Jesus called them, and at once they left the boat and their father, and went with Him. (Matthew 4:21-22)*

The New Testament records many examples of a close personal relationship between John and Jesus, such that John referred to himself on numerous occasions as ...*the one whom Jesus loved.* (*John 13:23*)

John was present at many of the key moments during the ministry and Passion of Jesus, including His Transfiguration on Mount Tabor.

> *Jesus took with Him Peter, James and John, and led them up a high mountain, where they were alone. As they looked on, a change came over Jesus, and His clothes became shining white—whiter than anyone in the world could wash them. Then the three disciples saw Elijah and Moses talking with Jesus...Then a cloud appeared and covered them with its shadow, and a voice came from the cloud, "This is My own dear Son—listen to Him!" They took a quick look around but did not see anyone else; only Jesus was with them. (Mark 9:2-7)*

After Jesus, in the presence of his disciples (including John), cured the woman who had suffered for twelve years from heavy menstrual bleeding (*Mark 5:25-34),* He was approached by Jairus, a synagogue official, to heal his young daughter, who was gravely ill. When messengers arrived to announce that the child had died, Jesus ignored the news and continued on.

> *He did not let anyone else go on with Him except Peter and James and his brother John. They arrived at Jairus' house, where Jesus saw the confusion and heard all the loud crying and wailing. Jesus said... "The child is not dead—she is only sleeping".... He took her by the hand and said to her, "Talitha, koum," which*

> means, "Little girl, I tell you to get up!" She got up at once and started walking around. (Mark 5:37-42)

While all twelve of Jesus' Apostles accompanied Him most, if not all, of the time during His three years of ministry, there were certain revelations, such as those mentioned above, that were experienced only by a select few of Jesus' chosen disciples—and John was included in this number.

Certainly John was present—as were all Twelve Apostles—at both the Last Supper and Jesus' visit to Gethsemane following the Supper. When Jesus revealed at the Last Supper that He would be betrayed, John's own Gospel reveals that he himself asked Jesus to reveal the identity of His betrayer:

> *Jesus...was deeply troubled and declared openly, "I am telling you the truth: one of you is going to betray Me." The disciples looked at one another, completely puzzled about what He meant. One of the disciples, the one whom Jesus loved,* [John] *was sitting next to Jesus...and asked, "Who is it, Lord?" Jesus answered, "I will dip some bread in the sauce and give it to him; he is the man." So He took a piece of bread, dipped it, and gave it to Judas, the son of Simon Iscariot. (John 13:21-26)*

Following the Supper, all of the Apostles—with the exception of Judas Iscariot, who had already departed separately—accompanied Jesus to the Garden of Gethsemane. But even though all were present, Jesus again extended a special invitation to a select few, including John:

> *They came to a place called Gethsemane, and Jesus said to His disciples, "Sit here while I pray." He took Peter, James and John with Him. Distress and anguish came over Him, and He said to them, "The sorrow in My heart is so great that it almost crushes Me. Stay here and keep watch." (Mark 14:32-34)*

After Jesus' arrest, trial, scourging and crucifixion, it was the crucified Jesus Whose request of John most clearly demonstrated the close bond between them, when He asked John to care for His mother Mary.

> *Standing close to Jesus' cross were His mother, His mother's sister, Mary the wife of Clopas, and Mary Magdalene. Jesus saw His mother and the disciple He loved [John] standing there; so He said to His mother, "He is your son." Then He said to the disciple, "She is your mother." From that time the disciple took her to live in his home. (John 19:25-27)*

John's own Gospel account of Easter morning details the discovery of the empty tomb and John's faith response to this discovery.

> *Early on Sunday morning, while it was still dark, Mary Magdalene went to the tomb and saw that the stone had been taken away from the entrance. She went running to Simon Peter and the other disciple whom Jesus loved [John] and told them, "They have taken the Lord from the tomb, and we don't know where they have put Him!"*

> *Then Peter and the other disciple went to the tomb. The two of them were running, but the other disciple ran faster than Peter and reached the tomb first. He bent over and saw the linen cloths, but he did not go in. Behind him came Simon Peter, and he went straight into the tomb. He saw the linen cloths lying there and the cloth which had been around Jesus' head. It was not lying with the linen cloths but was rolled up by itself. Then the other disciple, who had reached the tomb first, also went in; he saw and believed.* (John 20:1-8)

It is clear from Scripture—both in John's own Gospel as well as in the accounts of the synoptic evangelists—that John held a special place in Jesus' heart. This does not mean, however, that John was immune from reprimand or further instruction from Jesus.

> *As the time drew near when Jesus would be taken up to heaven, He...set out on His way to Jerusalem. He sent messengers ahead of Him, who went into a village in Samaria to get everything ready for Him. But the people there would not receive Him...When the disciples James and John saw this, they said, "Lord, do you want us to call fire down from heaven to destroy them?" Jesus turned and rebuked them. [possibly adding "...the Son of man did not come to destroy men's lives, but to save them]* (Luke 9:51-55)

On another occasion, John's mother, thought to be named Salome, made a request of Jesus that drew the ire of the other Apostles, although it would be unfair to blame this on John.

> *Then the wife of Zebedee came to Jesus with her two sons, bowed before Him, and asked Him for a favor. "What do you want?" Jesus asked her. She answered, "Promise me that these two sons of mine will sit at Your right and Your left when You are King."*
>
> *"You don't know what you are asking for," Jesus answered the sons. "...I do not have the right to choose who will sit at My right and My left. These places belong to those for whom My Father has prepared them."*
>
> *When the other ten disciples heard about this, they became angry with the two brothers, So Jesus called them all together and said, "...if one of you wants to be great, he must be the servant of the rest...like the Son of Man, Who did not come to be served, but to serve and to give His life to redeem many people." (Matthew 20:20-28)*

The four Gospel accounts differ slightly in reporting the appearances Jesus made to His twelve disciples in the days after His Resurrection. Matthew and Mark record that Jesus instructed the women whom He encountered at His burial place to tell His disciples that He would go ahead of them to Galilee, where He would later meet them. John, of course, was included in this number.

Luke recounted a different description of the post-Resurrection appearances of Jesus. He wrote in *Luke 24:13-50* of an encounter between the risen Jesus and two of His disciples on the road from Jerusalem to Emmaus, a village seven miles west of Jerusalem. Luke related how the disciples failed to recognize Jesus until they stopped to dine and Jesus intoned a blessing and broke and distributed bread—at which point their eyes were opened and they recognized Him. In this account, Jesus disappeared and the disciples returned to Jerusalem where they excitedly explained to the eleven disciples what they had encountered.

> *They got up at once and went back to Jerusalem, where they found the eleven disciples gathered together... saying, "The Lord is risen indeed!" The two then explained to them how they had recognized the Lord when He broke the bread.*
>
> *While the two were telling them this, suddenly the Lord Himself stood among them and said to them, "Peace be with you." They were terrified, thinking they had seen a ghost. But He said to them, "Why are you alarmed? Why are these doubts coming up in your minds? Look at My hands and feet and see that it is I Myself." (Luke 24:33-39)*

In this account, Jesus appeared to His disciples in Jerusalem, rather than in Galilee. After eating with the disciples and further explaining the Scriptures and the role of the Messiah to them, Jesus led the disciples out of Jerusalem to Bethany, a village about 2 miles east of Jerusalem, where Jesus blessed them and ascended into heaven.

John's Gospel addresses the post-Resurrection appearances of Jesus quite differently. In his account, Jesus appeared to ten of the disciples who were sequestered behind locked doors in Jerusalem out of fear of the Jewish authorities.

> *Then Jesus came and stood among them. "Peace be with you," He said. After saying this, He showed them His hands and His side. The disciples were filled with joy at seeing the Lord...Then He breathed on them and said, "Receive the Holy Spirit. If you forgive people's sins, they are forgiven; if you do not forgive them, they are not forgiven." (John 20:19-23)*

Missing from this gathering was the Apostle Thomas, who refused to believe that Jesus had risen unless and until he could see the scars from the nails used to crucify Jesus. One week later, when Jesus reappeared, Thomas got his wish and turned from doubt to faith with the words:

> *My Lord and my God! (John 20:28)*

But John's Gospel, unlike the other three synoptic Gospels, records yet another visitation of Jesus, this time to seven of the Apostles, culminating in a peculiar misunderstanding about John himself.

> *After this, Jesus appeared once more to His disciples at Lake Tiberias... Simon Peter, Thomas (called the Twin), Nathanael (the one from Cana in Galilee), the sons of Zebedee [James and John], and two other disciples of Jesus were all together....They went out in a boat...but did not catch a thing...As the sun was rising, Jesus stood at the water's edge, but the disciples did not know that it was Jesus...He asked them... "Haven't you caught anything?" "Not a thing," they answered. He said to them, "Throw your net out on the right side of the boat, and you will catch some." So they threw the net out and could not pull it back*

> in, because they had caught so many fish. The disciple whom Jesus loved [John] said to Peter, "It is the Lord." (John 21:1-7)

Jesus had prepared a fire and invited the disciples to eat with Him. When they finished eating, Jesus asked Peter on three separate occasions if Peter loved Him. Peter responded in the affirmative each time, but was saddened that Jesus had asked him three times to profess his love. This is when the misunderstanding about John developed—and so ended the *Gospel of John*.

> *Peter turned around and saw behind him that other disciple whom Jesus loved [John]...and...asked Jesus, "Lord, what about this man?" Jesus answered him, "If I want him to live until I come, what is that to you? Follow me!"*
>
> *So a report spread among the followers of Jesus that this disciple would not die. But Jesus did not say he would not die; He said, If I want him to live until I come, what is that to you?" (John 21:20-23)*

According to Fr. George Poulos, author of the 2005 text *Orthodox Saints*, "John remained close to the Mother of the Savior throughout her lifetime and was at her side when she breathed her last on August 15, officiating at her burial in the Garden of Gethsemane, a spot made sacred by her Son years before. He was among the other disciples who discovered the empty tomb of Mary, who forty days after her death had been assumed into Heaven. With his promise to Jesus for his Mother's care fulfilled, St. John now turned his full attention to carrying the message of Jesus Christ to the spiritually darkened areas of the then known world, preaching throughout Asia Minor with a passion that won converts who formed a solid base for the New Faith. Unlike the other eleven apostles, all of whom were martyred in the name of Jesus Christ, John lived to the ripe age of 105, escaping the fate of his brother evangelists. This remarkable durability provided for one of the longest services on record in the cause of Christ, a service which carried over into the second century which establishes him as a record holder in conversions to Christianity. Some estimates have it that he was personally responsible for winning over close to 400,000 pagans to Christianity, a staggering figure considering that his audiences could never have been at best a few hundred and most of the time a lot less."

While tradition holds that John took Jesus' mother Mary to live in Ephesus, there seems to be no specific evidence to support this. It is likely that they remained in Jerusalem until Mary's death (hence her burial in the Garden of Gethsemane), at which point John embarked on his missionary crusade, spending a great deal of time in the company of Peter. Chapters 3 and 4 of *Acts* report their miracles and preachings in Jerusalem and chapter 8 describes the baptisms they performed in Samaria. According to Rev. Sabine Baring-Gould in his 1914 text *The Lives of the Saints*, "When he [John] went to Ephesus is uncertain. He was at Jerusalem fifteen years after Saint Paul's first visit there [*Acts 15:6*]. There is no trace of his presence there when Saint Paul was at Jerusalem for the last time. Tradition, more or less trustworthy, completes the history. Irenaeus says that Saint John did not settle at Ephesus until after the death of Saints Peter and Paul, and this is probable. He certainly was not there when Saint Timothy was appointed bishop of that place. Saint Jerome says that he supervised and governed all the Churches of Asia. He probably took up his abode finally in Ephesus in 97 CE. In the persecution of Domitian he was taken to Rome, and was placed in a cauldron of boiling oil, outside the Latin gate, without the boiling fluid doing him any injury. [Eusebius makes no mention of this. The legend of the boiling oil occurs in Tertullian and in Saint Jerome]. He was sent to labor at the mines in Patmos. At the accession of Nerva he was set free, and returned to Ephesus, and there it is thought that he wrote his gospel."

It has been estimated that John the Evangelist was born between 10 and 15 CE, which would most likely have made him a late teenager or early 20-something-year-old at the time of his calling by Jesus. If he did live to the age of 105, he would have outlived all of the other Apostles, especially as one who died of natural causes rather than from martyrdom. With most historians and theologians estimating the composition of the *Book of Revelation* as circa 95 CE, it would have been possible for John the Evangelist to have authored it at the approximate age of 80 or 85. In fairness, the date of 95 CE, while favored by most, is not unanimous. Other biblical historians offer alternative dates such as 54-68 CE (during the reign of the Emperor Nero), 69-79 CE (coinciding with the reign of Vespasian) and 81-96 CE (the latter years of the reign of Domitian). In each case, it is suggested that the content of *Revelation* was important as a source of comfort and encouragement to a Christian community victimized by Roman persecution, which was present during the reign of each of these emperors. Of course, if these earlier dates prove to be accurate, then it is a much younger John who authored *Revelation*.

So John of Patmos—if he were indeed John the Evangelist and Apostle of Jesus—would be the author of the *Gospel of John*, the *First, Second* and *Third Letters of John*, and the *Book of Revelation*, which has also been called the *Apocalypse of John*. Only Saints Paul and Luke authored larger segments of the New Testament.

It should be noted that many of the esteemed Church Fathers, including Justin Martyr, Irenaeus, Clement of Alexandria, Tertullian, Cyprian, and Hippolytus, believed that John of Patmos and John the Evangelist were one and the same. However, this was denied by other Fathers, including Denis of Alexandria, Eusebius of Caesarea, Cyril of Jerusalem, Gregory Nazianzen, and John Chrysostom. And the disagreement rages on to this day. So...

WHAT IF JOHN OF PATMOS WAS SOMEONE DIFFERENT?

While most theologians and biblical historians ascribe to the believe that John of Patmos and John the Evangelist *were* one and the same, the *New World Encyclopedia* offered the reminder that, "Many modern scholars—as well as a number of the early Church Fathers—hold that John of Patmos was a different person from the other writers of the Johannine literature."

The reasons for this belief varied and, of course, if this belief is true, then all of the biographical information about John the

Apostle already presented is irrelevant and inapplicable. But then the question arises—if John of Patmos was *not* John the Apostle, then who was he?

A second century group of Christians known as the Alogi ("Deniers of the Word") categorically rejected both the *Gospel of John* and the *Book of Revelation* as false—because of their divergence from the theology of the synoptic Gospels. They claimed that both books were written by Cerinthus, a Christian of the second half of the first century CE who was viewed by many of the Church Fathers as a Gnostic heresiarch. So this theory offers yet another view of the true identity of "John of Patmos."

Others rejected John of Patmos as the same man as John the Evangelist for literary reasons. A disciple of the Church Father Origen, named Dionysius of Alexandria, believed that there were a number of both theological and stylistic differences between the *Gospel of John* and *Revelation*. The *New World Encyclopedia* also explained that, "With the advent of modern biblical criticism, many scholars, both secular and Christian, came to believe that John the Evangelist (who wrote the *Gospel of John*), and John of Patmos were two separate individuals. They point to several lines of evidence suggesting that John of Patmos wrote only *Revelation*, not the *Gospel of John* or the *Epistles of John*. For one, the author of *Revelation* identifies himself as "John" several times, but the author(s) of the *Gospel of John* and the writer of the epistles of "John" never identify themselves by name. In contrast to the author of the *Gospel of John*, John of Patmos speaks very much as a Jewish Christian, referring to Jesus as He who "holds the key of David"

(*Revelation 3:7*) and the "Lion of the tribe of Judah, the Root of David." (*Revelation 5:5*) He also condemns the careless attitude of some of the Pauline churches who permitted eating food which had been offered to idols (*Revelation 2:14* and *2:20*). Moreover, for John of Patmos, the "elect" saints are not Gentile Christians but "144,000 from all the tribes of Israel," with 12,000 coming from each specifically-named tribe (*Revelation 7:4-8*). A great multitude of Gentiles "from every nation" are also included, but not among the 144,000 (*Revelation 7:9*). Also, while both the *Gospel of John* and the *Book of Revelation* liken Jesus to a lamb, they consistently use different words for lamb when referring to him—the Gospel uses *amnos*, *Revelation* uses *arnion*. Lastly, the *Gospel of John* is written in nearly flawless Greek, but *Revelation* contains grammatical errors and stylistic abnormalities which indicate its author was not as familiar with the Greek language as the Gospel's author."

So ultimately we've come full circle. John of Patmos may be John the Evangelist and Apostle. Then again, maybe he's not. Perhaps he was, in actuality, a Gnostic-oriented heretic named Cerinthus—and perhaps not. There is no hard biographical evidence to support any alternative identity, so all that is left to do is focus on the prophetic message of the *Book of Revelation* rather than on its author.

IS *REVELATION* REALLY PROPHETIC?

In calling the *Book of Revelation* an authentic message from God, the accuracy of this description is stated quite clearly in the opening words of its first chapter:

> *This book is the record of the events that Jesus Christ revealed. God gave Him this revelation in order to show to His servants what must happen very soon. Christ made these things known to His servant John by sending His angel to him, and John has told all that he has seen. This is his report concerning the message from God and the truth revealed by Jesus Christ.*
>
> *Happy is the one who reads this book, and happy are those who listen to the words of this prophetic message and obey what is written in this book. (Revelation 1:1-3)*

John, speaking of himself from a third-person perspective, states rather emphatically that he has been given a message from God via Jesus and His angel to pass along to his readers with the hope and expectation that they will obey God's requirements. He even refers to his words as a "prophetic message." It doesn't get more explicit than that!

What should be understood about the *Book of Revelation* is that its style of writing—called *apocalyptic*—is entirely unique to the *New Testament*. This same style of writing is found in several books of the *Old Testament*, such as in *Daniel* and *Ezekiel*, and is characterized by extensive and varied symbolism as well as by dreams and/or visions and visitation by heavenly beings such as angels. The United States Conference of Catholic Bishops offered a very comprehensive introduction to *Revelation* on its website (https://bible.usccb.org/bible/revelation/0), where it explains that, "The Apocalypse, or *Revelation to John*, the last book of the Bible, is one of the most difficult to understand because it abounds in unfamiliar and extravagant symbolism, which at best appears unusual to the modern reader. Symbolic language, however, is one of the chief characteristics of apocalyptic literature, of which this book is an outstanding example. Such literature enjoyed wide popularity in both Jewish and Christian circles from circa 200 BCE to 200 CE."

The USCCB continues, "This book contains an account of visions in symbolic and allegorical language borrowed extensively from the Old Testament, especially *Ezekiel, Zechariah*, and *Daniel*. Whether or not these visions were real experiences of the author or simply literary conventions employed by him is an open question. This much, however, is certain: symbolic descriptions are not to be taken as literal descriptions, nor is the symbolism meant to be pictured realistically. One would find it difficult and repulsive to visualize a lamb with seven horns and seven eyes; yet Jesus Christ is described in precisely such words (*Revelation 5:6*). The author used these images to suggest Christ's universal (seven) power (horns) and knowledge (eyes). A significant feature of apocalyptic writing is the use of symbolic colors, metals, garments (*Revelation 1:13–16; 3:18; 4:4; 6:1–8; 17:4; 19:8*), and numbers (*four* signifies the world, *six* imperfection, *seven* totality or perfection, *twelve* Israel's tribes or the apostles, *one thousand* immensity). Finally the vindictive language in the book (*Revelation 6:9–10; 18:1–19:4*) is also to be understood symbolically and not literally. The cries for vengeance on the lips of Christian martyrs that sound so harsh are in fact literary devices the author employed to evoke in the reader and hearer a feeling of horror for apostasy and rebellion that will be severely punished by God."

"The lurid descriptions of the punishment of Jezebel (*Revelation 2:22*) and of the destruction of the great harlot, Babylon (*Revelation 16:9–19:2*), are likewise literary devices. The metaphor of Babylon as harlot would be wrongly construed if interpreted literally. On the other hand, the stylized figure of the woman clothed with the sun (*Revelation 12:1–6*), depicting the New Israel, may seem to be a negative stereotype. It is necessary to look beyond the literal meaning to see that these images mean to convey a sense of God's wrath at sin in the former case and trust in God's providential care over the church in the latter."

"The *Book of Revelation* cannot be adequately understood except against the historical background that occasioned its writing. Like *Daniel* and other apocalypses, it was composed as resistance literature to meet a crisis. The book itself suggests that the crisis was ruthless persecution of the early church by the Roman authorities; the harlot Babylon symbolizes pagan Rome, the city on seven hills (*Revelation 17:9*). The book is, then, an exhortation and admonition to Christians of the first century to stand firm in the faith and to avoid compromise with paganism, despite the threat of adversity and martyrdom; they are to patiently await the fulfillment of God's mighty promises. The triumph of God in the world of men and women remains a mystery, to be accepted in faith and longed for in hope. It is a triumph that unfolded in the history of Jesus of Nazareth and continues to unfold in the history of the individual Christian who follows the way of the cross, even, if necessary, to a martyr's death."

"Though the perspective is eschatological—ultimate salvation and victory are said to take place at the end of the present age when Christ will come in glory at the parousia—the book presents the decisive struggle of Christ and His followers against Satan and his cohorts as already over. Christ's overwhelming defeat of the kingdom of Satan ushered in the everlasting reign of God *(Revelation 11:15; 12:10)*. Even the forces of evil unwittingly carry out the divine plan *(Revelation 17:17)*, for God is the sovereign Lord of history."

"The *Book of Revelation* had its origin in a time of crisis, but it remains valid and meaningful for Christians of all time. In the face of apparently insuperable evil, either from within or from without, all Christians are called to trust in Jesus' promise:

> *Behold, I am with you always, until the end of the age. (Matthew 28:20).*

Those who remain steadfast in their faith and confidence in the risen Lord need have no fear. Suffering, persecution, even death by martyrdom, though remaining impenetrable mysteries of evil, do not comprise an absurd dead end. No matter what adversity or sacrifice Christians may endure, they will in the end triumph over Satan and his forces because of their fidelity to Christ the Victor. This is the enduring message of the book; it is a message of hope and consolation and challenge for all who dare to believe."

There is no doubt that John was convinced that he had been entrusted by God with the task of delivering specific messages to the seven Christian communities in the Roman province of

Asia—churches with which he was already intimately involved. He had a vision of Jesus, and explained:

> ...the Spirit took control of me, and I heard a loud voice that sounded like a trumpet speaking behind me. It said, "Write down what you see, and send the book to the churches in these seven cities: Ephesus, Smyrna, Pergamum, Thyatira, Sardis, Philadelphia and Laodicea." (Revelation 1:10-11)

John went on to describe his vision of Jesus and the additional instructions he received directly from Him:

> I turned around to see Who was talking to me, and I saw seven gold lampstands, and among them there was what looked like a human being, wearing a robe that reached to His feet, and a gold band around His chest. His hair was white as wool, or as snow, and His eyes blazed with fire; His feet shone like brass that has been refined and polished, and His voice sounded like a roaring waterfall. He held seven stars in His right hand, and a sharp two-edged sword came out of His mouth. His face was as bright as the midday sun. When I saw Him I fell down at His feet like a dead man. He placed His right hand on me and said, "Don't be afraid! I am the first and the last. I am the living One! I was dead, but now I am alive forever and ever.
>
> I have authority over death and the world of the dead. Write, then, the things you see, both the things that are now and the things that will happen afterward." (Revelation 1:12-19)

In John's vision, the seven lampstands represented the seven Christian communities of Asia, and his initial words were directed specifically to them.

THE MESSAGES TO THE SEVEN CHURCHES

The first order of business in *Revelation* was for John to fulfill his obligation to deliver God's messages to these communities. These messages comprise the totality of Chapters 2 and 3. So, to the church at Ephesus, John wrote:

> *I know what you have done; I know how hard you have worked and how patient you have been ...you have suffered for My sake, and you have not given up. But this is what I have against you: you do not love Me now as you did at first. Think how far you have fallen! Turn from your sins and do what you did at first. (Revelation 2:2-5)*

The church community at Smyrna received this message:

> *I know your troubles; I know that you are poor, but really you are rich! I know the evil things said against you...Don't be afraid of anything you are about to suffer. The Devil will put you to the test by having some of you thrown into prison, and your trouble will last ten days. Be faithful to Me, even if it means death, and I will give you life as your prize of victory. (Revelation 2:9-10)*

To the church at Pergamum, John wrote:

You are true to Me, and you did not abandon your faith in Me even during the time when Antipas, My faithful witness, was killed...But there are a few things I have against you: there are some among you who...eat food that has been offered to idols and ...practice sexual immorality...Now turn from your sins! (Revelation 2:13-16)

The church at Thyatira read these words:

This is the message from the Son of God...I know what you do. I know your love, your faithfulness, your service and your patience. I know that you are doing more now than you did at first. But this is what I have against you: you tolerate that woman Jezebel, who calls herself a messenger of God. By her teaching she misleads My servants into practicing sexual immorality and eating food that has been offered to idols. (Revelation 18-20)

The Christian community at Sardis was told:

I know what you are doing; I know that you have the reputation of being alive, even though you are dead! So, wake up and strengthen what you still have before it dies completely. For I find that what you have done is not yet perfect in the sight of My God. Remember, then, what you were taught and what you heard; obey it, and turn from your sins. (Revelation 3:1-3)

It was to the church community at Philadelphia that John wrote:

> *This is the message from the One Who is holy and true. I know what you do; I know that you have a little power; you have followed My teaching and have been faithful to Me...I love you. Because you have kept My command to endure, I will also keep you safe from the time of trouble which is coming upon the world to test all the people on earth. (Revelation 3:7-10)*

Lastly, the Christian community at Laodicea was told:

> *I know what you have done; I know that you are neither cold nor hot. How I wish you were either one or the other! But because you are lukewarm, neither hot nor cold, I am going to spit you out of My mouth! You say, "I am rich and well off; I have all I need." But you do not know how miserable and pitiful you are! You are poor, naked and blind....Turn from your sins. Listen! I stand at the door and knock... (Revelation 3:15-20)*

APOCALYPTIC LITERATURE

As previously mentioned, the compositional style of *Revelation* is apocalyptic—the only book of the *New Testament* so written. It is of the same genre as portions of the *Old Testament* books of *Daniel* and *Ezekiel*, and is characterized by numerous symbols, visions and spiritual beings. Attempts to interpret the message(s) of *Revelation* have been made throughout the two millennia of church history with little to no agreement on the part of theologians and biblical scholars, but it is this apocalyptic style—very different from the other Johannine writings—that is employed in all of the remaining chapters.

While it would be arrogant and pointless to make yet another attempt to interpret Chapters 4 to 21, suffice it to say, as the U.S. Conference of Catholic Bishops has already concluded, that the people of John's era would have a far greater understanding and appreciation of John's symbolism and visions than we of a much later age, so the best we can do is as follows: first, offer a rough summary of John's visions and symbols for our own reflection and consideration, and second, review the various methods of interpretation that have been developed over the course of time to reveal the meaning of these visions and symbols.

THE ROUGH SUMMARY....

Most Biblical historians and theologians view chapters 4-22 of *Revelation* as the epicenter of John's apocalyptic style of writing and, chapter by chapter, they view John's images with a critical eye as they attempt to decipher their message.

In Chapter 4, John presents his vision of heaven in the presence of the Holy Spirit. He sees a throne with someone sitting on it —a person with a gleaming countenance, radiant as gems. Encircling this throne were 24 other thrones on which sat elders wearing white robes and crowns. Four other creatures surrounded the central throne—each with 6 wings, each covered with eyes, but each with a different appearance: as either a lion, a bull, a human being or an eagle. While these creatures sing unending songs of honor and thanksgiving to the One on the throne, the 24 elders prostrate themselves in abject worship. All the while, flashes of lightning and peals of thunder complete the vision.

Chapters 5 through 8 are a continuation of the vision begun in Chapter 4, with a tremendous emphasis placed on the opening of a scroll with seven seals that needed to be broken. At the opening of Chapter 5, the One sitting on the throne held a sealed scroll to be opened, yet no one was worthy enough to make the attempt. Then, one of the elders noticed:

> *Look! The Lion from Judah's tribe, the great descendant of David...can break the seven seals and open the scroll. (Revelation 5:5)*

John then described seeing a Lamb with seven horns and seven eyes standing at the throne and taking the scroll from the One as the assemblage around the throne—with harps and bowls of incense—sang a song of praise and exaltation as they were joined by millions of angels, earthly creatures and the dead. In Chapter 6 the Lamb broke open the first six seals of the scroll. The first four seals released four horses—first, a white horse with a rider holding a bow; second, a red horse with a rider who was presented with a sword; third, a black horse whose rider held a pair of scales; and finally a fourth, pale horse whose rider was named Death.

After the Lamb broke the fifth seal, John reported:

> *I saw underneath the altar the souls of those who had been killed because they had proclaimed God's word and had been faithful in their witnessing. They shouted in a loud voice, "Almighty Lord,*

> *holy and true! How long will it be until you judge the people on earth and punish them for killing us?" Each of them was given a white robe, and they were told to rest a little while longer...* (Revelation 6:9-11)

The opening of the sixth scroll at the end of Chapter 6 wreaked havoc throughout the globe. There was an earthquake accompanied by the sun turning black, the moon turning blood red, stars falling from the sky, mountains and islands moving from their places, and the people of the earth—from the rich and powerful to the lowly slaves—hiding themselves to escape the anger of the One and the Lamb.

Following the cataclysm erupting after the breaking of the sixth seal, John's vision shifted in Chapter 7. He saw four angels who had been given the power to damage the earth and the sea standing at the four corners of the earth, when a fifth angel appeared with instructions from God not to harm the earth until God's servants had been marked with a seal on their foreheads. John went on to say that:

> *The number of those who were marked with God's seal on their foreheads was 144,000. They were from the twelve tribes of Israel, 12,000 from each tribe: Judah, Reuben, Gad, Asher, Naphtali, Manasseh, Simeon, Levi, Issachar, Zebulun, Joseph and Benjamin.* (Revelation 7:4-8)

As John looked around, he saw an enormous multitude of people from every race and nation, dressed in white robes and holding palm branches. This great throng of people joined the angels, elders and heavenly creatures around the throne, where they prostrated themselves before God and worshiped Him. One of the elders explained to John that these were the people who survived terrible persecution and now serve the Lamb without end. They will always be protected by the Lamb, who will save them from every want, pain and sorrow.

It is in Chapter 8 that the seventh seal was broken by the Lamb, and this was followed by a period of silence. Seven angels were given trumpets and an eighth angel filled an incense container with fire from the altar before throwing it on the earth, causing thunder, lightning and an earthquake.

The first angel blew his trumpet, sending hail and fire, mixed with blood, to the earth. The second angel then blew his trumpet, and a huge mountain of fire was thrown into the sea. When the third angel sounded his trumpet, a large star dropped from the sky and fell on the rivers and springs. Chapter 8 ends when the fourth angel blew his trumpet, causing the sun, moon and stars to lose one-third of their brightness. The destruction that befell the earth and its creatures was beyond terrible, but the Chapter ended when an eagle, flying overhead, screeched loudly:

> *O horror! Horror! How horrible it will be for all who live on earth when the sound comes from the trumpets that the other three angels must blow! (Revelation 8:13)*

The fifth and sixth angels blew their trumpets in Chapter 9. The fifth released a star that opened earth's abyss and released locusts to torture—but not kill—the inhabitants of the earth who were without the mark of God's seal on their foreheads. The locusts wore crowns of gold and iron breastplates, with the faces of men with the teeth of lions and the hair of women.

The sixth angel perpetuated the second horror by blowing his trumpet to release four other angels whose task was to kill a third of all humanity. With them were released two hundred million mounted troops. The riders wore breastplates of red, blue and yellow, and their steeds had heads like lions, spewing fire, smoke and sulfur. The horses' tails were like snakes. In this vision John saw that the people who were not killed at this time continued to worship demons, practice idolatry, magic and sexual immorality, and murder and steal.

In Chapter 10, a mighty angel with a rainbow encircling his head and a face like the sun appeared from heaven and held a small scroll in his hand. A voice from heaven instructed John not to write about this. The angel announced:

> *There will be no more delay! But when the seventh angel blows his trumpet, then God will accomplish His secret plan, as He announced to His servants, the prophets. (Revelation 10:7)*

The same voice then told John to eat the scroll, which will taste like honey in his mouth but turn sour in his stomach—and then to proclaim God's message.

Chapter 11 seems especially enigmatic. It opens with John being instructed to measure the temple of Jerusalem and its altar, and being told that God would send to Jerusalem two witnesses dressed in sackcloth, who will proclaim God's message for 1,260 days. John was told further that:

> The two witnesses are the two olive trees and the two lamps that stand before the Lord of the earth. If anyone tries to harm them, fire comes out of their mouths and destroys their enemies...They have authority to shut up the sky so that there will be no more rain during the time they proclaim God's message. They have authority also over the springs of water, to turn them into blood; they have authority also to strike the earth with every kind of plague as often as they wish. (Revelation 11:4-6)

Following their proclamation of God's message, the two witnesses, according to *Revelation*, would be attacked and killed by a beast rising out of the abyss, and their bodies would lie in a street in Jerusalem, where people of all nations would celebrate their deaths, blaming them for much of the suffering of humanity. After three-and-a-half days, God would breathe life back into them and call them into heaven, which they would enter in a cloud. Upon their ascension, an earthquake of great intensity would shake the city and kill thousands. This was the second horror.

The sounding of the seventh trumpet ended Chapter 11 with loud voices from heaven crying out:

> The power to rule over the world belongs now to Our Lord and His Messiah, and He will rule forever and ever! (Revelation 11:15)

This proclamation was followed by the 24 elders prostrating themselves before God in solemn worship while God's temple in heaven was opened, the Covenant Box revealed, and flashes of lightning, thunderclaps, an earthquake and heavy hail adding to the majesty and gravity of the moment.

The imagery in Chapter 12 is perhaps the best known of all of the symbolism in *Revelation*. John reports that he saw this sight in the sky:

> *There was a woman, whose dress was the sun and who had the moon under her feet and a crown of twelve stars on her head. She was soon to give birth, and the pains and suffering of childbirth made her cry out. Another mysterious sight appeared in the sky. There was a huge red dragon with seven heads and ten horns and a crown on each of his heads....He stood in front of the woman, in order to eat her child as soon as it was born. Then she gave birth to a son, who will rule over all nations with an iron rod. But the child was snatched away and taken to God and His throne. The woman fled to the desert, to a place God had prepared for her, where she will be taken care of for 1,260 days. (Revelation 12:1-6)*

Immediately following the plight of the woman and her newborn child, John chronicles the war that erupted in heaven between the archangel Michael and his angels against the dragon and his angels. John identifies the dragon as:

> *...that ancient serpent, named the Devil, or Satan, who deceived the whole world. (Revelation 12:9)*

The dragon and his angels were defeated, banished from heaven, and thrown down to earth, where the dragon continued to pursue the woman unsuccessfully. However, it would appear this battle was, indeed, far from over:

> *The dragon was furious with the woman and went off to fight against the rest of her descendants, all those who obey God's commandments and are faithful to the truth revealed by Jesus. (Revelation 12:17)*

The entirety of Chapter 13 is devoted to the story of the "Two Beasts." The first beast, rising out of the sea, looked like a leopard with bear's feet and a lion's mouth. It had ten horns with crowns, and seven heads bearing names that insulted God. The dragon empowered the beast—and the whole earth worshiped both the dragon and the beast—except those whose names before the dawn of creation were written in the Lord's book of the living.

A second beast, rising from the earth, had two horns like those of a lamb. It performed miracles and supported the first beast, forcing all the people to be marked on their foreheads or right hands with a sign that represented the beast. The sign was "666."

Chapter 14 shifted John's attention to the sight of the Lamb on Mount Zion with the 144,000 people who were marked with His name. These were men who followed the Lamb while remaining virgins, speaking the truth, and being without fault.

John then saw three angels appear, one at a time. The first angel announced that the time had arrived for God to judge all people. The second angel announced that:

She has fallen! Great Babylon has fallen! She made all people drink her wine—the strong wine of her immoral lust! (Revelation 14:8)

The third angel announced the punishment that would befall those who followed and worshiped the beast:

Those who worship the beast and its image and receive the mark on their forehead or on their hand will themselves drink God's wine, the wine of His fury, which He has poured at full strength into the cup of His anger! All who do this will be tormented in fire and sulfur before the holy angels and the Lamb. The smoke of the fire that torments them goes up forever and ever. There is no relief day or night for those who worship the beast... (Revelation 14:9-11)

The scene again shifted and John witnessed three angels, two of whom held large sickles. The third angel instructed the ones with sickles to:

Cut the grapes from the vineyard of the earth, because the grapes are ripe. (Revelation 14:18)

So many "grapes" were thrown into the winepress of God's fury that the blood flowing out of the winepress caused a flood 200 miles long and 5 feet deep.

Seven angels with seven plagues appeared in the sky in Chapter 15 followed by those who had defeated the dragon and the beast. They stood by a sea of glass, and holding harps given to them by God, they sang songs in praise of God and the Lamb. The seven angels then emerged from the Sacred Tent in the temple in heaven. Dressed in white robes with gold bands around their chests, they received seven gold bowls filled with the anger of God.

These gold bowls fared prominently in Chapter 16, when the angels were instructed to pour out the contents of the bowls of anger on the earth. The first bowl caused painful sores to break out on the followers of the beast, and the second bowl, poured into the sea, turned the waters into blood, killing all of the creatures in the sea. The third angel poured the contents of his bowl into the rivers and springs, also turning them to blood as well. The fourth angel poured his bowl onto the sun, which was then empowered to burn with incredible heat those who opposed God, The contents of the fifth bowl were poured onto the throne of the beast, causing darkness and pain as well. But despite the pain caused by the fourth and fifth bowls, the followers of the beast still refused to turn away from their sins.

The sixth angel poured out his bowl on the Euphrates River, drying it up. Then John saw a new image:

> *I saw three unclean spirits that looked like frogs. They were coming out of the mouth of the dragon, the mouth of the beast, and the mouth of the false prophet. They are the spirits of demons that perform miracles. These three spirits go out to all the kings of the world, to bring them together for the battle on the great Day*

of Almighty God. Then the spirits brought the kings together in the place that in Hebrew is called Armageddon. (Revelation 16:13-16)

When the seventh angel spilled the contents of his bowl, he spilled it into the air. A loud voice cried out from the throne in the temple, saying "It is done!" and lightning, thunder and the worst earthquake the world has ever seen followed. All of the earth's cities were destroyed, islands and mountains vanished, and huge hailstones of up to one hundred pounds fell from the sky.

Unlike the previous chapters of apocalyptic writing (Chapters 4-16), Chapter 17 offers—through the words of an angel accompanying John—an interpretation of the images presented. This chapter introduces the "Famous Prostitute" and the punishment she has earned. The angel invited John:

Come, and I will show you how the famous prostitute is to be punished, that great city that is built near many rivers. The kings of the earth practiced sexual immorality with her, and the people of the world became drunk from drinking the wine of her immorality. (Revelation 17:1-2)

John was transported to the desert, where he saw a woman sitting on a red beast with seven heads and ten horns. She was dressed in purple and scarlet and wore jewelry of gold and precious gems. On her forehead was inscribed "Great Babylon, the mother of all prostitutes and perverts in the world." She held a gold cup filled with obscene and filthy things, and she was drunk—from the blood of Jesus' followers who had been killed. The angel then explained the image:

> *I will tell you the secret meaning of the woman...and the beast...That beast... lives no longer; it is about to come up from the abyss...it was once alive...but it will reappear. The seven heads are seven hills, on which the woman sits. They are also seven kings: five of them have fallen, one still rules, and the other one has not yet come...the beast is itself an eighth king who is ...going off to be destroyed. The ten horns...are ten kings who have not yet begun to rule...but will be given authority to rule...for one hour with the beast...They will fight against the Lamb, but the Lamb... with His ...faithful followers, will defeat them, because He is Lord of lords and King of kings...The ten horns you saw and the beast will hate the prostitute; they will take away everything she has and leave her naked; they will eat her flesh and destroy her with fire...The woman you saw is the great city that rules over the kings of the earth. (Revelation 17:7-18)*

Despite the interpretative assistance from the angel, the meaning of the symbols used in this vision have been analyzed in different ways throughout the two millennia of Church history. It would seem that the words of the angel suggest that some of the symbols represent people, things or events happening within the lifetime of John, while other symbols suggest future persons or events. This is one of the reasons why various theologians and biblical exegetes have proposed different methods of interpretation of *Revelation*, as the next section of this chapter will introduce.

Chapter 18 opens with yet another angel coming down from heaven and crying out in a loud voice:

> *She has fallen! Great Babylon has fallen! She is now haunted by demons and unclean spirits; all kinds of filthy and hateful birds live in her. For all the nations have drunk her wine—the strong wine of her immoral lust. The kings of the earth practiced sexual immorality with her, and the businessmen of the world grew rich from her unrestrained lust. (Revelation 18:2-3)*

A second voice from heaven then calls out an invitation to God's people to reject Babylon so as not to suffer the same punishments. The people are urged to pay back Babylon double for her iniquities—and to give her as much suffering and grief as Babylon treated herself to glory and luxury. John then spoke of the kings and businessmen and ship captains and passengers who mourned a "great" city, yet one that lost all of its wealth in just an hour as a result of God's punishment.

The ultimate fate of Babylon—the final "nail in her coffin"—concluded Chapter 18 when an angel hurled a large millstone into the sea with the following epitaph:

> *This is how the great city Babylon will be violently thrown down and will never be seen again. The music of harps and of human voices, of players of the flute and the trumpet will never be heard in you again! No workman in any trade will ever be found in you again; and the sound of the millstone will be heard no more! Never again will the light of a lamp be seen in you; no more will the voices of brides and grooms be heard in you. Your businessmen*

were the most powerful in all the world, and with your false magic you deceived all the peoples of the world. (Revelation 18:21-23)

Babylon was punished because the blood of God's prophets and faithful followers was found in the city—the blood of all those who had been killed.

The tone of Chapter 19 changed dramatically, as John heard the roar of a large crowd of people in heaven praising God for His power, glory and just punishments. The elders and four living creatures prostrated themselves in worship before God, Who sat upon His throne. John then heard a crowd intone:

"Praise God! For the Lord, our Almighty God, is King! Let us rejoice and be glad; let us praise His greatness! For the time has come for the wedding of the Lamb, and His bride has prepared herself for it. She has been given clean shining linen to wear." (The linen is the good deeds of God's people.) (Revelation 19:6-8)

These words and gestures of praise and worship gave way to a new image—that of a great leader atop his noble steed:

Then I saw heaven open, and there was a white horse. Its rider is called Faithful and True; it is with justice that he judges and fights his battles. His eyes were like a flame of fire, and he wore many crowns on his head....The robe he wore was covered with blood. His name is "The Word of God." The armies of heaven followed him, riding on white horses and dressed in clean white linen. Out of his mouth came a sharp sword, with which he will

> *defeat the nations. He will rule over them with a rod of iron, and he will trample out the wine in the winepress of the furious anger of the Almighty God. On his robe and on his thigh was written the name: "King of kings and Lord of lords." (Revelation 19:11-16)*

In the battle that followed, with the beast and the kings of the earth and their armies clashing with the "King of kings and Lord of lords," the beast and the false prophet who supported him were thrown alive into a lake of fire while their armies were slain by the sword that came out of the mouth of the rider of the white horse, and birds consumed their flesh.

Chapter 20 introduces an angel who holds in his hand the key to the abyss along with a heavy chain. He seizes the dragon… that is the Devil, or Satan—and locks him in the abyss for one thousand years. Then the souls of the dead who had followed Jesus and rejected the beast came to life to rule as kings with Jesus.

After a millennia has passed, Satan will be set loose to deceive the nations of the world, but he and his followers will be destroyed by fire from heaven, and the Devil will be thrown into the same lake of fire as the beast and his false prophet, to be tormented day and night, forever and ever. Chapter 20 ends with "The Final Judgment"—John now sees a great white throne in front of which were standing those awaiting judgment. These were judged according to their deeds, and those whose names were not recorded in the book of the living were thrown into the lake of fire.

Again the tone shifts as Chapter 20 leads into Chapter 21—judgment gives way to redemption. John described his new vision by revealing:

> *I saw the Holy City, the new Jerusalem, coming down out of heaven...I heard a loud voice speaking from the throne: "Now God's home is with mankind! He will live with them, and they shall be His people...He will wipe away all tears from their eyes. There will be no more death, no more grief or crying or pain. (Revelation 21:2-4)*

John then received specific instructions from God:

> *Write this, because these words are true and can be trusted...It is done! I am the first and the last, the beginning and the end. To anyone who is thirsty I will give the right to drink from the spring of the water of life...Whoever wins the victory will receive this from Me: I will be his God, and he will be My son. But cowards, traitors, perverts, murderers, the immoral, those who practice magic, those who worship idols, and all liars—the place for them is the lake burning with fire and sulfur... (Revelation 21:5-8)*

An angel then told John that he would show him "the Bride, the wife of the Lamb" and transported him to a high mountain from which he saw the new Jerusalem descending from heaven. John described it:

> *The city shone like a precious stone...clear as crystal. It had a great high wall with twelve gates...On the gates were written the names of the twelve tribes...of Israel....The city's walls were built on twelve*

foundation stones on which were written the names of the twelve apostles of the Lamb...

> *The city was perfectly square...it was fifteen hundred miles long... the wall was 216 feet high...made of pure jasper, and the city itself was made of pure gold...the foundation stones...were adorned with all kinds of precious stones...the twelve gates were twelve pearls...The city has no need of the sun or the moon...because the glory of God shines on it...Only those whose names are written in the Lamb's book of the living will enter the city. (Revelation 21:10-27)*

Chapter 22 ends the *Revelation* of John of Patmos. The angel proceeded to show John the river of the water of life which flows from God's throne down the middle of the city's street. On each side of the river was the tree of life, which blossoms every month. Everyone will see the face of God, Whose name will be written on each forehead. Night will be no more—nor will there be need of lamps or sunlight, because the Lord God will be their light forever.

The angel instructed John:

> *Do not keep the prophetic words of this book a secret, because the time is near when all this will happen..."Listen," says Jesus. "I am coming soon! I will bring My rewards with me, to give to each one according to what he has done. I am the first and the last, the beginning and the end...I, Jesus, have sent My angel to announce these things to you in the churches. I am descended from the*

family of David; I am the bright morning star." (Revelation 22:10-16)

And John ended this prophetic book with the following blessing and warning:

> I, John, solemnly warn everyone who hears the prophetic words of this book: if anyone adds anything to them, God will add to His punishment the plagues described in this book. And if anyone takes anything away from the prophetic words of this book, God will take away from him his share of the fruit of the tree of life and of the Holy City, which are described in this book. He Who gives His testimony to all this says, "Yes, Indeed. I am coming soon!" So be it. Come, Lord Jesus. May the grace of the Lord Jesus be with everyone. (Revelation 22:18-21)

Given the wide variety and complexity of the symbols and images used by John throughout the apocalyptic writings of *Revelation*, it should come as no surprise to even the most casual of readers that so many of John's images and symbols are open to a great many disparate interpretations. It may seem pretty clear to some that John uses "the Lamb" to represent Jesus, but what about so many of the others: the dragon, the beast, the woman in scarlet and purple, seven seals, trumpets and bowls—just to name a few? What is the significance of certain numbers and colors? What about the scrolls, plagues, Babylon, the wedding and the white rider? So many have tried to make lasting sense out of these images, but the meaning behind many of them remains a mystery two millennia later. However, it may be of interest to investigate the four primary "schools" or methods of interpretation that have been offered for our consideration throughout the history of the Church.

THE FOUR METHODS OF INTERPRETATION

In 2016, Pastor Christopher L. Scott of Lakeview Missionary Church in Moses Lake, Washington, pointed out in his internet blog that, "About twenty-five years ago upwards of five hundred works attempting to interpret the book of *Revelation* were on file in the British Museum. One man examined them all and testified that no two of them exactly agreed." Pastor Scott went on to outline four different methods that have been used by scholars and theologians to interpret the words of *Revelation* and attempt to make sense of its apocalyptic symbolism and imagery. These methods are known as the historicist, preterist, idealist and chiliastic methods.

In the **Historicist** view, the symbols and images are making predictions about upcoming events in human history—from the lifetime of John of Patmos up to the age of the historicist theologian. Apologist Patrick Zukeran, co-author of *The Apologetics of Jesus*, explained, "This view teaches that *Revelation* is a symbolic representation that presents the course of history from the Apostle's life through the end of the age. The symbols in the apocalypse correspond to events in the history of western Europe, including various popes, the Protestant Reformation, the French Revolution, and rulers such as Charlemagne. Most interpreters place the events of their day in the later chapters of *Revelation*. Many adherents of this position view chapters 1-3 as seven periods in church history. The breaking of the seals in chapters 4-7 symbolizes the fall of the Roman Empire. The Trumpet judgments in chapters 8-10 represent the invasions of the Roman Empire by the Vandals, Huns, Saracens, and Turks. Among Protestant Historicists of the Reformation, the antichrist in *Revelation* was believed to be the papacy. Chapters 11-13 in *Revelation* represent the true church in its struggle against Roman Catholicism. The bowl judgments of *Revelation* 14-16 represent God's judgment on the Catholic Church, culminating in the future overthrow of Catholicism depicted in chapters 17-19.

Of course, there are very many who strongly disagree with this particular interpretation (including a great many Catholics!), and one of the major criticisms of the Historicist View is that its interpretation—over the course of time—must necessarily shift to accommodate the most recent historical developments. Christopher L. Scott concluded, "The historicist interpretation makes sense when applied to the letters to the seven churches in *Revelation 2-3*, however this is a difficult interpretation to hold for *Revelation 4-19*. Within this view the beast/Antichrist has been identified as the Pope, Napoleon, Mussolini, and Hitler. The main weakness of this view is that it has to reinterpret the book of *Revelation* for every new period of history. Few people take this position today."

The second method of interpretation, the **Preterist** view, is, perhaps, best outlined by Dr. Gavin Ortlund, pastor of the First Baptist Church in Ojai, California, who explained, "Preterism is well defined at theopedia.com as 'a view in Christian eschatology which holds that some or all of the biblical prophecies concerning the Last Days refer to events which took place in the first century after Christ's birth, especially associated with the destruction of Jerusalem in 70 CE. The term preterism comes from the Latin *praeter*, meaning past, since this view deems certain biblical prophecies as past, or already fulfilled.'"

According to Pastor Ortlund, there are several variations in the preterist philosophy. Full preterists believe that all eschatological events were fulfilled in the first century, and we are now living in the new heavens and the new earth. For full preterists, Jesus' second coming was not a bodily and visible return at the end of history, but a spiritual return manifested in judgment on Jerusalem via the Roman army in 70 CE. Full preterists also believe the final resurrection took place "spiritually" during the first century. Full preterism is viewed as heretical by most conservative Christians and creedally heterodox by all Christians (including most full preterists themselves). Partial preterists believe that prophecies concerning the destruction of Jerusalem, the great tribulation, the antiChrist, and a "judgment coming" of Christ were fulfilled during the Roman siege of Jerusalem culminating in the destruction of the temple in 70 CE. Textually, partial preterists view the Olivet Discourse (*Matthew 24, Mark 13, Luke 21*) and the majority of the book of *Revelation* as referring to first century events. Partial preterists maintain, however, that the second coming (bodily and undeniable), the final judgment, the final resurrection, and the inauguration of the new heavens and new earth await future fulfillment. Partial Preterists are almost always amillennialists or postmillennialists. With regard to *Revelation*, this means that chapters 1-19 (in the partial preterist view) are primarily concerned with first century events—events that most of John's original readers would experience within their lifetime.

The **Idealist** view, unlike both the historicist and preterist philosophies, does not tie the visions and symbols of *Revelation* to specific events in history, According to Methodist pastor Daniel Humbert, "The idealist view does not take a literal historical or futuristic fulfillment but sees the entire book as a symbolic presentation of the battle between good and evil...The symbols in *Revelation* are not tied to specific events but point to themes throughout church history. The seals, bowls, and trumpets speak repeatedly to the events of human history in every age and give believers of all ages an exhortation to remain faithful in the face of suffering. The battles in *Revelation* are viewed as spiritual warfare manifested in the persecution of Christians or wars in general that have occurred in history. The beast from the sea may be identified as the satanically inspired political opposition to the church in any age. The beast from the land represents pagan, or corrupt, religion to Christianity. Catastrophes represent God's displeasure with sinful man; however, sinful mankind goes through these catastrophes while still refusing to turn and repent. God ultimately triumphs in the end."

Early Church Fathers such as Origen and St. Augustine embraced this interpretation. Its greatest asset is making the symbolism of *Revelation* relevant to Christians of all ages and backgrounds, rather than tying them to specific moments in history.

The fourth method of interpretation is the **Chiliastic**, or **Futurist**, view of *Revelation*, which is traced back to a Jesuit priest of the 16th century, Rev. Francisco Ribera. Daniel Humbert upholds that, "The futurist view sees everything beginning with chapter four and onward as yet to be fulfilled in our future.

Futurists divide the book of *Revelation* into three sections based on 1:19: "what you have seen, what is now, and what will take place later." Chapter 1 describes the past ("what you have seen"), Chapters 2-3 describe the present ("what is now"), and the rest of the book describes future events ("what will take place later")."

"Futurists argue that a consistently literal or plain interpretation is to be applied in understanding the book of *Revelation*. Chapter 4:1 is the rapture of the church to heaven. Chapters 4-19 refer to a period known as the seven-year tribulation (*Daniel 9:27*). During this time, God's judgments are poured out upon mankind as they are revealed in the seals, trumpets, and bowls. Chapter 13 describes a literal future world empire headed by a political leader called the Antichrist, which is pictured by a Beast. Chapter 19 refers to Christ's second coming and the battle of Armageddon. This is followed by a literal thousand-year rule of Christ upon the earth in chapter 20. Chapters 21-22 are events that follow the millennium: the creation of a new heaven and a new earth and the arrival of the heavenly city upon the earth."

As you can see, there is no unanimity among Christian theologians as to the best, or most accurate, way to interpret the words, visions and symbolism used in *Revelation*. Apocalyptic literature, by its very nature, lends itself to a variety of different interpretations by the images and symbols it employs. The purpose of this book is not to endorse or disparage any one of these methods of interpretation—historicist, preterist, idealist or futurist—but rather to determine if John of Patmos can appropriately be labeled a prophet of God.

CHAPTER 10: QUESTIONS FOR REVIEW

1. What evidence is there to support the belief that John of Patmos and John the Evangelist were the same person?
2. What reasons do theologians give for believing John of Patmos and John the Evangelist are two different people?
3. What were the two circumstances that got John and James into trouble with Jesus and the other apostles?
4. What special responsibility did Jesus entrust only to John?
5. When did Jesus appear to John in the days after His Resurrection?
6. What is it about *Revelation* that theologians consider it a prophetic writing?
7. What is the common thread that runs through the messages that John offers to the seven Christian communities in the Province of Asia?
8. What are the usual characteristics of *apocalyptic* literature? Where else does this style of writing appear in the Bible?
9. Of all of the symbols and images used by John in Chapters 4-22, which three do you think are the easiest to interpret? Which three are the most difficult?
10. What are the four methods of interpretation of Revelation that are in use today? Briefly describe each.

Chapter Eleven
PHILIP THE EVANGELIST AND HIS FOUR DAUGHTERS

"We stayed at the house of Philip the evangelist...
He had four unmarried daughters who proclaimed God's message"

Certain names pop up throughout the New Testament and it becomes necessary to differentiate one Mary from another, one Judas from another, and so on and so on. Such is the case with Philip. Philip "the Evangelist" was *not* the brother of Herod Antipas and ruler of Iturea and Trachonitis, nor was he one of Jesus' twelve Apostles. Rather, he is first mentioned in *Acts of the Apostles*, where he was chosen, along with seven others, to resolve a dispute that had emerged in the church in Jerusalem:

> *As the number of disciples kept growing, there was a quarrel between the Greek-speaking Jews and the native Jews. The Greek-speaking Jews claimed that their widows were being neglected in the daily distribution of funds. So the twelve apostles called the whole group of believers together and said, "It is not right for us to neglect the preaching of God's word in order to handle finances. So then, brothers, choose seven men among you who are known to be full of the Holy Spirit and wisdom, and we will put them in charge of this matter. We ourselves, then, will give our full time to prayer and the work of preaching."*
>
> *The whole group was pleased with the apostles' proposal, so they chose Stephen, a man full of faith and the Holy Spirit, and Philip and Prochorus, Nicanor, Timon, Parmenas, and Nicolaus, a Gentile from Antioch who had earlier been converted to Judaism. The group presented them to the apostles, who prayed and placed their hands on them. (Acts 6:1-6)*

When Stephen addressed the Sanhedrin and accused them of betraying and murdering God's "righteous Servant," the furious Council members dragged him out of the city and stoned him to death. This marked the beginning of a large-scale persecution of the Christian community in Jerusalem.

> *All the believers, except the apostles, were scattered throughout the provinces of Judea and Samaria...Saul tried to destroy the church; going from house to house; he dragged out the believers, both men and women, and threw them into jail. (Acts 8:1-3)*

The believers who scattered to other towns and provinces did not do so primarily out of fear. They used this opportunity to spread the word of the risen Christ to other communities. And such was the case with Philip:

> *Philip went to the principal city in Samaria and preached the Messiah to the people there. The crowds paid close attention to what Philip said, as they listened to him and saw the miracles that he performed. Evil spirits came out from many people with a loud cry, and many paralyzed and lame people were healed. So there was great joy in the city. (Acts 8:5-8)*

Certainly Philip must have been called by the Holy Spirit to perform the miraculous acts ascribed to him above, but his success at conveying the Gospel message went even further, as displayed in two additional stories about Philip. The first is a continuation of his efforts in Samaria:

> *A man named Simon lived there, who for some time had astounded the Samaritans with his magic. He claimed that he was someone great, and everyone in the city, from all classes of society, paid close attention to him. "He is that power of God known as 'The Great Power,'" they said. They paid this attention to him because for such a long time he had astounded them with his magic. But when they believed Philip's message about the good news of the Kingdom of God and about Jesus Christ, they were baptized, both men and women. Simon himself also believed; and after being baptized, he stayed close to Philip and was astounded when he saw the great wonders and miracles that were being performed. (Acts 8:9-13)*

Missionary evangelist Daniel King pointed out in his 2017 monograph, that when "Philip preached to the Samaritans; this was a revolutionary act in his time. Traditionally the Jews and the Samaritans had no contact with one another. They hated each other. Yet, Philip broke tradition and went to those who were different. In doing this, he followed the example of his master, Jesus, who had ministered to the Samaritan woman at the well *(John 4)*. When the Samaritans accepted the Gospel, it was a great breakthrough because it proved that Christ is for the whole world, not just the Jews.

Philip's success in Samaria was followed by a revelation that took him elsewhere:

> *An angel of the Lord said to Philip, "Get ready and go south to the road that goes from Jerusalem to Gaza."...So Philip got ready and went. Now an Ethiopian eunuch, who was an important*

official in charge of the treasury of the queen of Ethiopia, was on his way home. He had been to Jerusalem to worship God and was going back home in his carriage. As he rode along, he was reading from the book of the prophet Isaiah. The Holy Spirit said to Philip, "Go over to that carriage and stay close to it." Philip ran over and heard him reading from the book of the prophet Isaiah. He asked him, "Do you understand what you are reading?"

The official replied, "How can I understand unless someone explains it to me?" And he invited Philip to climb up and sit in the carriage with him. The passage of scripture which he was reading was this:

"He was like a sheep that is taken to be slaughtered, like a lamb that makes no sound when its wool is cut off. He did not say a word. He was humiliated, and justice was denied him. No one will be able to tell about his descendants, because his life on earth has come to an end."

The official asked Philip, "Tell me, of whom is the prophet saying this? Of himself or of someone else?" Then Philip began to speak; starting from this passage of scripture, he told him the Good News about Jesus. As they traveled down the road, they came to a place where there was some water, and the official said, "Here is some water. What is to keep me from being baptized?"

The official ordered the carriage to stop, and both Philip and the official went down into the water, and Philip baptized him. When they came up out of the water, the Spirit of the Lord took Philip away. The official did not see him again, but continued on his way, full of joy. Philip found himself in Azotus; he went on to

> *Caesarea, and on the way he preached the Good News in every town. (Acts 8:26-40)*

Philip's evangelism, as recorded in *Acts*, ends with his conversion of the Ethiopian eunuch. The only other time his name appears in *Acts* is much later—perhaps as much as twenty years later, by some estimates—when he played host to Paul during Paul's third missionary journey, circa 54-55 CE:

> *We continued our voyage, sailing from Tyre to Ptolemais, where we greeted the believers and stayed with them for a day. On the following day we left and arrived in Caesarea. There we stayed at the house of Philip the evangelist, one of the seven men who had been chosen as helpers in Jerusalem. He had four unmarried daughters who proclaimed God's message. (Acts 21:7-9)*

Please note that the closing words in the citation above are translated as "four unmarried daughters who proclaimed God's message" while the *New American Bible* (like many other translations) offers the alternative translation *"four unmarried daughters gifted with prophecy."* It is on the basis of the *New American Bible* use of the word "prophecy" that these four women are included in this text.

Philip is the only person throughout the *New Testament* who is referred to as an "evangelist," (rather than as a "prophet") but exactly what an "evangelist" is and does is never really specified. Contemporary radio evangelist Lawrence Dubois pointed out in his 2021 monograph "Evangelist Emeritus" that "the term evangelist was used to describe all preachers of the good news...There are those whose entire ministry is devoted to preach the gospel and bring the opportunity of salvation to the unsaved. Philip is the only *New Testament* example we are given of this ministry."

In the text of the *New Testament,* Philip is not called a "prophet" per se, but does the designation fit him for his inclusion in this text? After all, Paul, in discussing the various ministries in the early Church, differentiated between prophets and evangelists:

> He [Jesus] appointed some to be apostles, others to be prophets, others to be evangelists, others to be pastors and teachers. (Ephesians 4:11)

However, if Lawrence Dubois' definition is accurate and an evangelist such as Philip is chosen by Jesus to deliver the message of "Good News" to provide an opportunity for salvation for others, then his evangelistic ministry clearly fits the generic definition of a prophet as one who delivers God's messages to His people.

How interesting it is, then, to read that Philip's four daughters *are* referred to as prophets. However, except for that single statement to that effect in *Acts 21,* no other mention is made of Philip's daughters, much less the message(s) they were expected to deliver to God's people. Therefore, it becomes necessary to search outside the *New Testament* to find additional material about them.

Scriptural writer Mark Carlson-Ghost, in his 2016 monograph "Philip's Daughters, Great Lights of the Early Church," pointed out that "If you do a superficial search of the internet about Philip's daughters, you often find statements that the names of these women were never given. That isn't the case, though the names given in historical accounts are not always consistent. One source names three of them: Hermione, Eutychis [Eutychiane or Eukhidia]...A third sister is named Irais, and the fourth may be Chariline."

In her 2021 text *Women of Faith and Courage: Stories of Women in the Bible and History*, Christian writer Mary Walker thought that Luke's inclusion of the four daughters of Philip in his *Acts* was especially significant for the larger lesson it taught. "These women were examples given to us by Luke that there were some changes in the new religion known as 'The Way.' Christian disciples will be made up of men and women. Women will be allowed to do many things that they were denied in Judaism. When the Holy Spirit came He gave gifts, including prophecy, to men and women. The Gospel will transform lives—religiously and socially. Women will no longer be second-class citizens. They will do their part in the life of the Church."

HERMIONE

On the strength of the writings of various non-scriptural authors and historians, probably more is known about Hermione than her other sisters. She is venerated as a saint in both the Roman Catholic and Orthodox Churches, and her feast day is celebrated on September 4th.

Hermione is often referred to as "Hermione of Ephesus," although she apparently grew up in Caesarea. While in Caesarea she studied the medicinal arts in the hope that she would be able to provide healing and comfort for her neighbors. This vocation may have been inspired by her father Philip, whose responsibilities were to provide compassion and a fair disbursement of finances to meet the needs of the widows of his church community. Shortly after Paul visited the house of Philip in Caesarea, anti-Christian Roman forces drove many in the Christian community out of their homes and neighborhoods. Philip's family, along with many others, fled Caesarea and took refuge in the inland city of Hierapolis in present-day Turkey. It is unclear how long Hermione may have resided in Hierapolis, but according to Orthodox Protopresbyter Fr. George Papavarnavas, at some point Hermione and her sister Eutychis traveled to Ephesus, a bustling seaport on the west coast of Turkey, where they underwent theological training under Petronios, who was a disciple of the Apostle John.

Hermione remained in Ephesus, where she bought a house and opened a clinic to care for the poor and homeless. She later expanded her clinic to include extra rooms for the homeless and travelers—creating a hospital-hotel known as a *xenodochia*. Merging her medical skills with her faith in Jesus, Hermione's fame as a healer began to spread beyond Ephesus throughout Asia Minor, ultimately incurring the wrath of pagans who brought her before the Roman Emperor Trajan, who was passing through Ephesus en route to a military campaign against the Persians. Trajan initially tried to persuade Hermione to renounce her faith, but she remained steadfast. Angered by her bold proclamation of faith in Jesus, Trajan ordered that Hermione should be beaten—struck repeatedly in the face over a period of several hours. But Hermione, comforted by a vision of the Lord sitting upon His throne, endured this beating with great courage, and then prophesied to Trajan, under the inspiration of the Holy Spirit, that he would be victorious in his battle with the Persians. Whether or not Trajan had faith in Hermione's prophetic utterance is unknown, but he was nevertheless pleased with her prediction—and allowed her to go free.

This was not Hermione's only encounter with an Emperor of Rome. As Fr. Papavarnavas explained, "Hermione continued to preach the Gospel and to heal people until she was arrested again by Hadrian, Trajan's son-in-law and successor, who ordered her to be tortured harshly. They threw her into a cauldron with boiling molten tar and sulfur, but she remained unharmed. They then placed her on a frying pan. When they once again saw that she was invulnerable, they brought her to the pagan temple to sacrifice to idols, but the idols fell and self-demolished. Then they attempted to behead her, but this did not take place because the hands of the two executioners, Theodoulos and Theotimos, became paralyzed. The Saint healed them and they confessed their faith in Christ, which they sealed with the blood of their martyrdom. And before other executioners arrived to behead her, Christ received her holy soul, and her body was buried by the faithful of Ephesus."

It is thought that Hermione may have been buried in Ephesus on the eastern slope of Pion Hill, which is purported to be the burial site of Mary Magdalene, her father Philip and Saint

Timothy, but there is no archaeological evidence (yet) to support this conclusion. Others believe that Hermione may have been buried either in Hierapolis or Caesarea.

Because she was well-known for her healing skills, St. Hermione (also spelled Ermioni) is the patron of healers, and has been approached by the faithful with this prayer:

> O glorious Saint Hermione,
> You served God in humility and confidence on earth
> Now you enjoy His Beatific Vision in heaven.
> You persevered in death and gained the crown of eternal life.
> Remember now the dangers and confusion and anguish that surround me in this vale of tears,
> And intercede for me in my needs and troubles, especially _____. Amen.

While it is possible to find some biographical information about Hermione from non-scriptural sources, uncovering similar information about her three sisters is far more elusive and scarce.

EUTYCHIS (EUTYCHIANE OR EUKHIDIA)

Whether she is referred to as Eutychis, Eutychiane or Eukhidia, sources indicate that Hermione's sister spent time with Hermione in care of the sick and homeless in Ephesus, approximately from 105 CE. However, it should be made clear that Eutychis (despite the similarity in the spelling of their names) is *not* the young man raised from the dead by Paul in Troas in the previous chapter of *Acts*:

> On Saturday evening we gathered together for the fellowship. Paul spoke to the people and kept on speaking until midnight, since he was going to leave the next day. Many lamps were burning in the upstairs room where we were meeting. A young man named Eutychus was sitting in the window, and as Paul kept on talking, Eutychus got sleepier and sleepier, until he finally went sound asleep and fell from the third story to the ground. When they picked him up, he was dead. But Paul went down and threw himself on him and hugged him. "Don't worry," he said, "he is still alive!" Then he went back upstairs, broke bread, and ate. After talking with them for a long time, even until sunrise, Paul left. They took the young man home alive and were greatly comforted. (Acts 20:7-12)

Similarly, Eutychis is not the archimandrite Eutyches who denounced the teachings of Nestorius in 431 CE at the First Council of Ephesus.

Tradition maintains that Eutychis (as mentioned above) accompanied her sister Hermione to Ephesus to meet John of Patmos in the hope of aiding him in his evangelization efforts. Upon hearing that John had died, they studied instead with his disciple Petronios. Hermione's medical skills led her to open a clinic and temporary dwelling for the ill and travelers in Ephesus, an enterprise with which she was aided by her sister Eutychis. Neither the Bible nor alternative non-scriptural sources offer much more information specific to Eutychis, except to suggest that she was buried either in Ephesus or Caesarea. Both Hermione and Eutychis are mentioned by name in the *Menaion*, which is the name of the twelve books that contain the offices for immovable feasts in the Byzantine Orthodox rite.

IRAIS AND CHARILINE

According to Mark Carlson-Ghost, Irais and Chariline were the two daughters of Philip who remained with him in the city of Hierapolis in Phrygia, while Hermione and Eutychis settled in Ephesus. Papias was the Bishop of Hierapolis and author of one of the earliest histories of the infant Church, but while the complete text of his history has been lost, a number of excerpts have been found in the writings of other historians, such as Eusebius. In his *Historia Ecclesiastica*, Eusebius reported that Papias described how people would travel long distances to hear Irais and Chariline relate their knowledge of the early church. Papias also mentioned, without specifying the identity, that one of the sisters actually rose from the dead.

In his 2020 monograph, Carlson-Ghost also raised—and answered the question—"How is it that these marvelous details are so little known? Apparently left unnoticed by most writers on the subject, Papias' account creates an evocative image of Irais and Chariline, two female elders of the early Christian church, highly respected by their male bishop and sought after by Christians far and wide. Unfortunately, on the unnamed person who rose from the dead, and the specific prophetic abilities and activities of the two sisters, the existing record is silent.

Like their father and sisters in Ephesus, Irais and Chariline may also have devoted themselves to acts of healing and charity. Many travelers came to the springs of Hierapolis for their healing properties and the two sisters may have included attention to physical as well as spiritual matters. It also seems likely that their prophetic gifts led them to do more than just share captivating stories of the past but also offer spiritual insights and teaching for the present. Whatever the case, the historical shadow cast by Irais and Chariline has just grown considerably longer."

WHY THE REFERENCE?

Many Biblical scholars have raised the question as to the reason Luke mentioned and identified Philip's daughters as both virgins and prophets. Please note that at the beginning of this chapter, the exact citation from the *Good News Bible* that is serving as the Scriptural reference text for this book translates the Greek as "four unmarried daughters who proclaimed God's message" while many other translations of *Acts* employ the words "four virgins who prophesied." Sometimes alternative translations can make a great deal of difference.

Luke's inclusion of this reference to Philip's daughters has been interpreted in several different ways. One theory is that it allows him to "tip his hat" to them for providing Luke with important details that he included in his writing. Biblical scholar Frederick Fyvie Bruce, in his 1988 text *The Book of Acts:*

New International Commentary on the New Testament, suggested that "The daughters, or at least some of them, lived to a great age, and were highly esteemed as informants on persons and event belonging to the early years of Judaean Christianity. It has been surmised that information such as Philip and his daughters could supply was highly prized by Luke who made use of it in the composition of his twofold history [the *Gospel of Luke* and *Acts of the Apostles*]—not only during the few days which he spent at Caesarea...but also during the two years of Paul's imprisonment there."

The generation of Church leaders following the Apostles needed to continue the work of evangelization and dissemination of the Good News that was begun by their predecessors. To that extent, Australian theologian Mary Mowczyko wrote in her 2013 monograph "Philip's Prophesying Daughters" that "The histories of Eusebius and Nicephorus associate the daughters of Philip with apostolic gifts, teaching, and foundational ministry. Like the prophets Judas and Silas who are mentioned in *Acts*, Philip's four daughters probably had much to say that encouraged and strengthened the believers in the early church...Eusebius regarded Philip's daughters and their ministry as the benchmark for prophetic ministry in the early church, and he implies that Philip's daughters...took over from the apostles' ministry."

The *Gospel of Luke* and *Acts* placed great emphasis on Jesus' sensitive and compassionate treatment of women in an age and culture when a prevailing patriarchy limited their impact and influence on Judean society. Biblical Scholar and pastor Dr. Christopher Smith saw this inclusion as yet another indication that the gifts of the Holy Spirit are meant for men and women alike. He wrote. "Early in the book, Luke records how the Holy Spirit descended on the young community on the day of Pentecost and enabled its members to speak all the different languages of the visitors who had come to Jerusalem for that festival. That was a picture of how the community would spread to people of all backgrounds. To explain to the crowd that gathered what was happening, the apostle Peter quoted these words from the prophet Joel: "In the last days, God says, I will pour out My Spirit on all people. Your sons and daughters will prophesy, your young men will see visions, your old men will dream dreams. Even on My servants, both men and women, I will pour out My Spirit in those days, and they will prophesy." [Joel 2:28-29] The Pentecost episode is like an overture, encapsulating the themes that play out in the rest of the book. The prophetic gifting and ministry of Philip's daughters is a fulfillment of the words, "Your ... daughters will prophesy." So I think that when Luke was putting together the book under divine inspiration, he recognized that staying in their house and witnessing them using this gift was not just a memorable personal experience, but something that he should share with his readers as an example of how the words of Joel continued to come true as the Holy Spirit empowered the community of Jesus' followers—men and women, young and old, of different social classes—to spread the good news."

CHAPTER 11: QUESTIONS FOR REVIEW

1. What is the controversy surrounding the identity of the *New Testament* Philip whose four daughters were called "prophets?"
2. What miracles were performed by Philip the Evangelist?
3. What was the nature of the relationship between Philip and Simon the Magician and the Ethiopian eunuch?
4. Philip is described as an "evangelist"—but is he also a prophet?
5. What was unusual about Philip's decision to spread the Good News in Samaria?
6. Why is there more information about Hermione than about her other sisters?
7. Which of Philip's daughters established themselves in Ephesus and which daughters remained in Hierapolis?
8. Why did Luke mention Philip's daughters in *Acts 21*—and why did he specify that they were both unmarried (virgins) and prophets?

Chapter Twelve
THE TWELVE

"These twelve men were sent out by Jesus with the following instructions...'Go and preach the Kingdom of God is near'..."

Many different words have been used to describe the followers of Jesus who put their faith in Him and tried to follow the message of His Good News once they recognized Him as the Messiah, the Son of God. They've been called His disciples, followers of "The Way" and "Christians" - and these earliest followers have been similarly categorized according to the way they were gifted by the Holy Spirit:

> *There are different abilities to perform service, but the same God gives ability to all for their particular service. The Spirit's presence is shown in some way in each person for the good of all. The Spirit gives one person a message full of wisdom, while to another person the same Spirit gives a message full of knowledge. One and the same Spirit gives faith to one person, while to another person He gives the power to heal. The Spirit gives one person the power to work miracles, to another the gift of speaking God's message, and to yet another, the ability to tell the difference between gifts that come from the Spirit and those that do not. To one person He gives the ability to speak in strange tongues, and to another he gives the ability to explain what is said. But it is one and the same Spirit Who does all this; as He wishes. He gives a different gift to each person. (1 Corinthians 12:6-11)*

As the early church grew and began to organize itself structurally, some of these special gifts of the Spirit evolved into functional roles, as some disciples assumed the role of elders, presbyters, deacons (and deaconesses), evangelists and prophets - among others. But what about the Twelve Apostles, called by Jesus to be His closest associates? Are they in a class by themselves - head and shoulders above all of the other disciples? Should they also be labeled "prophets" - or is their unique role in salvation history so extraordinary and special that the designation "prophet" is inapplicable, perhaps even beneath them?

We have previously discussed the Old Testament understanding of the role of "prophet" as one who serves as a messenger for God - delivering whatever message God wishes to convey to whatever audience He chooses at whatever time He decides. And we similarly discussed that the New Testament understanding of "prophet" may actually be more expansive - incorporating pastoral, proclamatory and interpretive functions above and beyond the responsibilities of a simple message delivery service. So the question remains: are the Apostles *prophets*?

We are very familiar with the names of the Twelve, and we are equally aware that several of them are more prominently featured throughout the four Gospels. About several we have detailed information, and with others we are left largely in the dark.

> *Jesus called His twelve disciples together and gave them authority to drive out evil spirits and to heal every disease and every sickness. These are the names of the twelve apostles: first Simon (called Peter) and his brother Andrew; James and his brother John, the sons of Zebedee; Philip and Bartholomew; Thomas and Matthew, the tax collector; James, son of Alphaeus, and*

Thaddeus; Simon the Patriot, and Judas Iscariot, who betrayed Jesus. (Matthew 10:1-4)

According to St. John, Andrew was the first Apostle to follow Jesus after hearing John the Baptist call Jesus "the Lamb of God." *(John 1:34-40)* Andrew then introduced his brother Simon to Jesus, Who looked at him and said:

Your name is Simon, son of John, but you will be called Cephas. [This is the same as Peter and means "a rock."] (John 1:42)

Both Matthew and Mark, however, offer identical accounts of Jesus' simultaneous call to Andrew and Simon as they were fishing:

As Jesus walked along the shore of Lake Galilee, He saw two brothers who were fishermen, Simon (called Peter) and his brother Andrew, catching fish in the lake with a net. Jesus said to them, "Come with Me and I will teach you to catch men." At once they left their nets and went with Him. (Matthew 4:18-20)

Luke's account is slightly different, with Jesus speaking only to Peter, whose fishing expedition on Lake Gennesaret had been unsuccessful until Jesus made a suggestion that reaped an incredibly large catch of fish for Simon and his partners James and John. Andrew is not mentioned in Luke's account *(Luke 51-11)* at all.

The three synoptic Gospels mention James and John, the sons of Zebedee, as the next Apostles called by Jesus but, according to John:

> *The next day* [the day after Jesus called Andrew and Simon] *Jesus decided to go to Galilee. He found Philip and said to him, "Come with Me!" (Philip was from Bethsaida, the town where Andrew and Peter lived.) Philip found Nathanael* [also known as Bartholomew] *and told him, "We have found the One Whom Moses wrote about in the book of the Law and Whom the prophets also wrote about. He is Jesus, son of Joseph, from Nazareth. (John 1:43-45)*

Matthew, Mark and Luke all agree that the next Apostle called by Jesus was Levi, also known as Matthew:

> *Jesus went back again to the shore of Lake Galilee. A crowd came to Him, and He started teaching them. As He walked along, He saw a tax collector, Levi, son of Alphaeus, sitting in his office. Jesus said to him, "Follow Me." Levi got up and followed Him. (Mark 2:13-14)*

THE INNER SANCTUM

These five Apostles - Simon (Peter), Andrew, James, John and Matthew are the only Apostles whose occupations are specified in Scripture - the first four being fishermen and Matthew serving as a tax collector. Of these five, three comprised what might be called Jesus' "inner sanctum" - they were called by Jesus to witness events in His life to which the other Apostles weren't party. Simon Peter, James and John - but not Simon Peter's brother Andrew - were present when Jesus raised from the dead the young daughter of Jairus, the synagogue official:

> *When He arrived at the house [of Jairus], He would not let anyone go in with Him except Peter, John and James, and the child's father and mother. Everyone there was crying and mourning for the child. Jesus said, "Don't cry; the child is not dead - she is only sleeping!" They all made fun of Him because they knew that she was dead. But Jesus took her by the hand and called out, "Get up, child!" Her life returned and she got up at once, and Jesus ordered them to give her something to eat. (Luke 8:51-55)*

Likewise, these same three were invited by Jesus to bear witness to a theophanic moment known as the *Transfiguration*:

> *Six days later Jesus took with Him Peter and the brothers James and John and led them up a high mountain where they were alone. As they looked on, a change came over Jesus: His face was shining like the sun, and His clothes were dazzling white. Then the three disciples saw Moses and Elijah talking with Jesus. So Peter spoke up and said to Jesus, "Lord, how good it is that we are here! If You wish, I will make three tents here, one for You, one for Moses, and one for Elijah."*
>
> *While he was talking, a shining cloud came over them, and a voice from the cloud said, "This is My own dear Son, with Whom I am pleased. Listen to Him!" When the disciples heard the voice they were so terrified that they threw themselves face downward*

on the ground. Jesus came to them and touched them. "Get up," He said. "Don't be afraid!" So they looked up and saw no one there but Jesus. (Matthew 17:1-8)

One other instance when these three Apostles were accorded special intimacy occurred when Jesus and the Twelve visited the Garden of Gethsemane after the Last Supper.

Then Jesus went with His disciples to a place called Gethsemane, and He said to them, "Sit here while I go over there to pray." He took with Him Peter and the two sons of Zebedee. Grief and anguish came over Him, and He said to them, "The sorrow in My heart is so great that it almost crushes Me. Stay here and keep watch with Me." (Matthew 26:36-38)

THE OTHERS

As far as the remaining Apostles are concerned, the New Testament offers little to no personal information about their respective calls to Apostleship or the details of their lives. There are no Scriptural records of their ages, occupations or marital status. And obfuscation about their lives is compounded by the fact that they are often called by different names. Simon, as mentioned, is called "Cephas" by Jesus, but he is popularly known as Peter, since Peter, like Cephas, means "rock." The brothers James and John are frequently labeled the "sons of Zebedee" - but Jesus nicknamed them the "Sons of Thunder." Since there is a second James among the Twelve Apostles, this "other" James is often referred to as James, the "son of

Alphaeus" or "James the Lesser" or "James the Younger" to avoid confusion.

The Synoptic evangelists call the next Apostle Bartholomew, but John refers to him as Nathaniel or Nathanael. Thaddeus is also called "Jude," "Jude Thaddeus" or "Judas Thaddeus" so as not to confuse him with Judas Iscariot, who betrayed Jesus. Thomas was also called "Didymus" - both Thomas and Didymus alternative translations for the word "twin." And the other Simon (not Simon Peter) is variously called "Simon the Zealot," "Simon the Patriot" or "Simon the Canaanite."

Although the Gospels chronicle the presence of all twelve Apostles throughout the three years of Jesus' public ministry and specify their unanimous presence at the Last Supper, in the Garden of Gethsemane, in the upper room in Jerusalem after Jesus' Resurrection as well as on the Day of Pentecost, little to no additional biographical information exists in the New Testament to "flesh them out."

Various extratestamental sources offer what is largely approximate information about their lives and ministries after Jesus' Ascension. For example, it is assumed that all of the Apostles, except John the Evangelist, who lived into his nineties, were martyred. Judas Iscariot, of course, can be thought of as self-martyring.

It is generally assumed that Peter, after spreading the Good News in Samaria and Asia Minor, died in Rome, circa 64-68 CE. His brother Andrew carried the Gospel message into Greece, Turkey and Eastern Europe, until his death in 60 CE. James, the brother of John, died rather early in 44 CE after evangelizing as far away as Spain. No records exist - even approximations - about Matthew, but it is thought he spread the Good News into Syria, Persia, Media, Parthia and Ethiopia. Similarly, there are no records of the death dates of Batholomew (Nathaniel) or Thaddeus (Jude, Judas), but Bartholomew evangelized in Armenia, Persia and India, while Thaddeus did the same in Syria, Mesopotamia and Armenia, as well.

James, the son of Alphaeus, is thought to have been martyred in Egypt, circa 62 CE while Simon the Zealot may have been killed in 65 CE in either Egypt or Persia. "Doubting" Thomas spread the Word of Jesus in Parthia, Persia and India, suffering death in 72 CE, and Philip evangelized in Syria, Asia Minor and Greece before succumbing in 80 CE.

All of the above information about dates and ministerial settings is conjectural at best but, on a more basic level, the specific details are irrelevant. Jesus called all of His Apostles - His closest friends and confidants - to deliver God's message to His people. That simple fact makes each Apostle who spread His Gospel message a bonafide prophet. As such, each of them has a place of importance in this text. (Well, not Judas Iscariot!) Interestingly enough, each of the synoptic Evangelists who recorded Jesus' commissioning of the Apostles as messengers of the Word expressed the call differently. Matthew wrote:

> *These twelve men were sent out by Jesus with the following instructions...Go and preach "The Kingdom of heaven is near!" Heal the sick, bring the dead back to life, heal those who suffer from dreaded skin diseases. And drive out demons. (Matthew 10:5-8)*

Mark recorded:

> *Then Jesus...called the twelve disciples together and sent them out two by two...They went out and preached that people should turn away from their sins. They drove out many demons and rubbed olive oil on many sick people and healed them. (Mark 6:7, 12-13)*

Luke chronicled:

> *Jesus called the twelve disciples together and gave them power and authority to drive out all demons and to cure diseases. Then He sent them out to preach the Kingdom of God and to heal the sick...The disciples left and traveled through all the villages, preaching the Good News and healing people everywhere. (Luke 9:1-2, 6)*

And finally, the Gospel of Matthew sealed Jesus' call to the Apostles when it ended with the following command of Jesus:

> *Jesus drew near and said to them, "I have been given all authority in heaven and on earth. Go, then, to all peoples everywhere and make them My disciples: baptize them in the name of the Father, the Son, and the Holy Spirit, and teach them to obey everything I have commanded you. And I will be will you always, to the end of the age." (Matthew 28:18-20)*

CHAPTER 12: QUESTIONS FOR REVIEW

1. In what way do the Twelve Apostles meet the definition of the word *prophet*?
2. Who were members of Jesus' "inner sanctum?" What experiences did they have that were not shared by the other Apostles?
3. What were the occupations of the Apostles? Whose occupations are unknown to us?
4. What message(s) did Jesus entrust to His Apostles to convey to the people?
5. Why is there some confusion about the names and identities of some of the Apostles? Be specific.
6. How do each of the synoptic Gospel writers describe the message of Jesus the Apostles were asked to bring to others?

BIBLIOGRAPHY

Anderson, Karl. "Simeon Niger." June 16, 2020 https://heritagelutheran.org/2020/06/16/simeon-niger/

Baring-Gould, Sabine. *The Lives of the Saints*. Edinburgh: Hodges and Sons Printers. 1914

Beare, Frank W. *St. Paul and His Letters* Nashville: Abingdon Press 1962

Blaylock, Richard. "Toward a Definition of New Testament Prophecy" *Themelios*, December 2022, https://www.thegospelcoalition.org/themelios/author/richard-blaylock/

Bouchard, Karen Scalf. "7 Things You Probably Didn't Know About John the Baptist." *Biblica*. January 14, 2021. https://www.biblica.com/articles/7-things-you-probably-didnt-know-about-john-the-baptist/

Boyer, James L. "The Office of the Prophet In New Testament Times." *Grace Journal* GJ 01:1. Spring 1960

Branch, Robin Gallaher. "Anna in the Bible." *Bible History Today* August 7, 2022 https://www.biblicalarchaeology.org/daily/people-cultures-in-the-bible/people-in-the-bible/anna-in-the-bible/

Bruce, Frederick Fyvie. *The Book of Acts: New International Commentary on the New Testament*. William B. Eerdmans Publishing Co. June 30, 1988

Busenitz, Nathan. "Five Dangers of Fallible Prophecy." March 1, 2012 https://thecripplegate.com/five-dangers-of-fallible-prophecy/

Cachila, JB. "Who is Agabus in the *Book of Acts* and what can we learn from him?" April 10, 2018. https://www.christianitytoday.com/article/who-is-agabus...

Carlson-Ghost, Mark. "Philip's Daughters, 'Great Lights' of the Early Church." 2016. https://www.markcarlson-ghost.com/index.php/2016/09/17/philips-daughters-prophets-names/

Cobb, Bradley. "Who was Judas Barsabbas?" December 16, 2015 https://thecobbsix.com/who-was-judas-barsabbas/

Dahl, Nils. *Studies in Paul*. Minneapolis:Augsburg Publishing House. 1977

Doyle-Nelson, Theresa. "St. Manaen—A Friend to St. John the Baptist's Murderer." *National Catholic Register*. May 24, 2019. https://www.ncregister.com/blog/st-manaen-a-friend-to-st-john-the-baptist-s-murderer

Driscoll, Mark. "Continuationism vs. Cessationism." 2022. https://realfaith.com/daily-devotions/continuationism-vs-cessationism/

Dubois, Lawrence. "Evangelist Emeritus." 2021 http://www.lawrencedubois.com/

Franciscan Foundation for the Holy Land. "The Importance of John the Baptist." https://ffhl.org/importance-john-baptist/

Geisler, Norman and Zukerman, Patrick. *The Apologetics of Jesus*. Baker Publishing. January 2009

Good News Bible with Deuterocanonicals/Apocrypha. New York: American Bible Society. 1976

Hill, David. *New Testament Prophecy*. Atlanta: John Knox. 1979

Humbert, Danuel. "The Four Views of Revelation." November 4, 2021 https://www.tmumc.org/stories/posts/the-four-views-of-revelation

Jackson, Wayne. "Who Was John the Baptist?" *Christian Courier.com*. June 23, 2022 https://www.christiancourier.com/articles/266-who-was-john-the-baptist

King, Daniel. "Lessons from the Life of Philip the Evangelist." Global Network of Evangelists. December 5, 2017. https://www.evangelist.global/resources/blog/lessons-from-the-life-of-philip-the-evangelist-2/

Kosobucki, David. "Simon of Cyrene and Simeon Called Niger." January 16, 2019. https://davidkosobucki.com/2019/01/16/simon-of-cyrene-and-simeon-called-niger-2/

Lioy, Dan. "Barnabas: 43 Facts and Lessons from the Life of a Disciple." disciplr.com/barnabas-facts-lessons

Myers, Jacob M. and Freed, Edwin D. "Is Paul Also Among the Prophets?" *Interpretation: A Journal of Bible and Theology*. November 5, 2016. https://journals.sagepub.com/doi/abs/10.1177/002096436602000104

McDaniel, Debbie. "6 Powerful Truths from the Life of John the Baptist That Offer Hope for Today." *Crosswalk.com*. February 10, 2021 https://www.crosswalk.com/faith/women/6-powerful-truths-from-the-life-of-john-the-baptist-that-offer-hope-for- today.html

Mowczko, Marg. "Philip's Prophesying Daughters." November 24, 2013. https://margmowczko.com/philips-prophesying-daughters/

New American Bible. New York: Benziger Inc. 1970

New World Encyclopedia. Prentice Hall. 1993

O'Neal, Sam. "Who Was Simeon Niger in the Bible?" February 6, 2019 https://www.learnreligions.com/who-was-simeon-niger-in-the-bible-363316

Orr, Adam. "Manaen—An Unlikely Teacher." December 4, 2020. https://westsidechristians.org/manaentheteacher/

Ortlund, Gavin. "Reflections on Revelation (2): A Brief Introduction to Preterism." June 25, 2008 https://gavinortlund.com/2008/06/25/reflections-on-revelation-2-a-brief-introduction-to-preterism/

Papavarnavas, George. "St. Hermione the Prophetess as a Model for our Lives." September 4, 2015. https://www.johnsanidopoulos.com/2015/09/saint-hermione-prophetess-as-model-for.html

Pierre, Archbishop Christophe. "Address to the Plenary Assembly of the U.S. Conference of Catholic Bishops." June 16, 2021. https://www.usccb.org/resources/21-Archbishop%20Christophe%20Pierre%20Address%20at%20General%20Assembly%20(06.16.21)_0.pdf

Poulos, George. *Orthodox Saints*. Holy Cross Orthodox Press. 2005

Richards, Sue and Larry. *Every Woman in the Bible.* Nashville: Thomas Nelson Publishers. 1999

Sanford, David. "Who was Barnabas in the Bible?" February 18, 2021 https://www.christianity.com/wiki/people/who-was-barnabas-in-the-bible.html

Scott, Christopher L. https://christopherscottblog.com/ 2016

Seitz, Christopher R. *Prophecy and Hermeneutics:Toward a New Introduction to the Prophets,* Grand Rapids: Baker Publishing Group. 2007

Sisters of St. John the Baptist. "Who is St. John the Baptist?" https://baptistines.org/st-john-the-baptist

Smith, Christopher R. "Why Does Luke Mention Philip's Daughters?" January 31, 2021. https://goodquestionblog.com/2021/01/31/why-does-luke-mention-phillips-daughters/

Staniforth, Maxwell and Louth, Andrew. *Early Christian Writings: The Apostolic Fathers.* Penguin UK. 1987

Stewart, Don. "Who Were the New Testament Prophets?" *Blue Letter Bible.* March 23, 2022 https://www.blueletterbible.org/faq/don_stewart/don_stewart_389.cfm

Storms, Sam. "What Does Scripture Teach About the Office of Prophet and Gift of Prophecy?" *NIV Zondervan Study Bible.* Zondervan. 2015

Swiatocho, Kris. "The Women in Christ's Life: Anna the Prophetess." *The Singles Network Ministries.* https://www.thesinglesnetwork.org/uploads/4/6/4/9/4649501/prophetess.pdf

Tashjian, Jirair. "John the Baptist: The Man and His Influence." *The Voice.* Christian Resource Institute. 2018. https://www.crivoice.org/johnbaptist.html

"The Gospel of Barnabas—What is It?" Got Questions Ministries. n.d. https://www.compellingtruth.org/gospel-of-Barnabas.html

Tibbs, Clint. "Religious Experience of the Pneuma." *WUNT* 2/230. 2007 https://www.mohrsiebeck.com/en/monograph-series/wissenschaftliche-unter suchungen-zum-neuen-testament-wunt-i

US Conference of Catholic Bishops. https://bible.usccb.org/bible/revelation/0. 2023

Walker, Mary. *Women of Faith and Courage: Stories of Women in the Bible and History.* Christian Faith Publishing. 2021

ABOUT THE AUTHOR

Kieran Larkin has been teaching theology for over 40 years in high school and college. He holds a B.A. in Religious Studies from St. Francis College in Brooklyn and an M.A. in Education from NYU. His two previous books, *Messengers of God: A Survey of Old Testament Prophets* and *Women Prophets of the Old Testament* received awards from the Catholic Press Association, and *Prophets of the New Testament: Before, During and After Jesus* completes this trilogy about a remarkable and inspirational cadre of people—men and women alike—who answered the call of the Lord with a faith and devotion that is truly beyond human understanding.

www.ingramcontent.com/pod-product-compliance
Lightning Source LLC
Chambersburg PA
CBHW060557080526
44585CB00013B/604